scaling

conversations

DAVE MACLEOD

scaling

conversations

HOW LEADERS
ACCESS THE
FULL POTENTIAL
OF PEOPLE

WILEY

Published by John Wiley & Sons, Inc., Hoboken, New Jersey.
Published simultaneously in Canada.

For general information on our other products and services or for technical support, please contact our Customer Care Department within the United States at (800) 762-2974, outside the United States at (317) 572-3993 or fax (317) 572-4002.

Wiley publishes in a variety of print and electronic formats and by print-on-demand. Some material included with standard print versions of this book may not be included in e-books or in print-on-demand. If this book refers to media such as a CD or DVD that is not included in the version you purchased, you may download this material at http://booksupport.wiley.com. For more information about Wiley products, visit www.wiley.com.

Library of Congress Cataloging-in-Publication Data

Names: Macleod, Dave (Chief executive officers), author.
Title: Scaling conversations : how leaders access the full potential of people / Dave Macleod.
Description: Hoboken, New Jersey : Wiley, [2021] | Includes index.
Identifiers: LCCN 2021008933 (print) | LCCN 2021008934 (ebook) | ISBN 9781119764458 (hardback) | ISBN 9781119764519 (adobe pdf) | ISBN 9781119764502 (epub)
Subjects: LCSH: Business communication. | Conversation.
Classification: LCC HF5718 .M3175 2021 (print) | LCC HF5718 (ebook) | DDC 658.4/5–dc23
LC record available at https://lccn.loc.gov/2021008933
LC ebook record available at https://lccn.loc.gov/2021008934

Cover Art and Design: Paul McCarthy

SKY10025770_032421

For and because of my amazing boys Aaron, Liam, and Fynn

CONTENTS

THE LIMIT OF OUR COMPETITIVE ADVANTAGE

We humans are uniquely wired for empathy, facial recognition, and language. Our ability to collaborate with one another, beyond our relative groups, is widely recognized as the key ingredient of what has driven so much of our amazing progress as a species. Long ago humans were, fortunately, able to recognize the mutual benefit of our interdependence. Rather than just brutally compete with each other at all times, we took an interest in the well-being of others to improve our own lives. Initially we applied this to feeding ourselves and to simple ways of interacting beyond our family members. Over time, we developed deeper and deeper ways of collaborating more effectively. Again, for our own gain.

As our societies developed, we were pretty successful at collaboration: We embraced our ability to empathize and consider the points of view of others; we leveraged our ability to recognize each other and remember who we had made agreements with; and we refined our language to improve how we created things that mutually benefitted all of us. Soon enough we spread to all corners of the planet and created a global ability to share our feelings and opinions, watch sports and buy things from one another, using screens in our pockets. The language and technology we use to better cooperate with one another continues to evolve to this day as we all keep working to solve problems that threaten our species in small and large ways.

It would be great if we could simply spend a lot of time discovering and celebrating our incredible ability to work together as a species, but unfortunately, and obviously, we have used those same abilities to divide and polarize.

Along with our favorable wiring, as a species we are also wired in extremely unhelpful ways. Often described as two different "kinds of brain," along with our ability to learn and be creative, we have parallel survival instincts that hijack our capacity to empathize and communicate effectively. When we perceive a threat, humans react similarly to many other animal groups: We respond by fighting, fleeing or freezing. This happens in both well- and less-understood ways.

On the well-understood side, sometimes relatively simple "threats" can cause two perfectly reasonable adults to be suddenly angry and unable to inhabit the same room. Sometimes, reading an email or social post that seems threatening can destroy an entire relationship. Different views on religion, philosophy and politics can make people so divided they can't even hear one another, never mind collaborate. You can easily think of hundreds of human behaviors that decrease our ability to work well together.

On the less-understood side, unconscious biases can cause people to misinterpret and react poorly to one another based on things they don't clearly realize. Extroverts and introverts require different environments to allow effective communication. Systemic racism has created mechanisms to ensure privileged people have more ability to influence than people with a different skin color. Social media is built to silo people and amplify extreme voices in an echo chamber.

For nearly every communication ability we can point to, as a species, we can also single out a failure to communicate that threatens our organizations, our society and, ultimately, our world. The remedy for this is to continue to improve our ability to share our voice, listen to one another, and discover common ground and insight to our mutual benefit. Simply, we need to converse better.

Over the years, humans have innovated to overcome our unfavorable wiring and our inability to converse in large groups. To try to ensure we get as much benefit as possible from group conversations we have invented talking sticks, council etiquette, and, in more recent times, *Robert's Rules of Order*—an adaptation of the rules and practice of Congress to address the needs of non-legislative societies published by US Army Officer Henry Martyn Robert in 1876. Many organizations train people in collaborative negotiation, conflict resolution and group meeting facilitation. Recognizing our inability to converse effectively in large groups, leaders in all sectors of society try to add structures to get the best out of groups and avoid the worst behaviors and outcomes.

The problem is that none of these systems scale up.

The talking stick, and its culture of respecting every voice, is probably still the most effective invention but doesn't help a group that can't sit together. Our current attempts at scaling communications digitally, to include many people, give unfair voice to small groups, divide people into silos, and create echo chambers within threads and channels of similarly minded people.

The communication challenges facing our organizations and our society are increasingly urgent and we need to focus on what has always given us an advantage as a species: Our ability to converse. As a leader, you need to improve your ability to lead mutually beneficial interactions in which people feel heard, insights emerge, and trust increases. Our organizations are getting more complex, our population is growing, and therefore our ability to converse effectively needs to scale just as fast, or faster.

I'm currently the CEO of a fast-growing technology company in the conversation space, but I didn't grow up in tech. Quite the opposite. As a young adult living in British Columbia, Canada, I worked for many years in the late 1990s and early 2000s as an experiential educator and an outdoor adventure guide at a place called Educo Adventure School. As a group of young leaders, tasked with carrying the flame of an outdoors school founded in the early 1960s, we did our best to draw out the unique leadership qualities of young people as we climbed ropes and mountains, experienced sweat lodges with Secwepemc leaders and explored group communication through good times and challenges. While the rappelling, climbing, zip-lining and river-paddling provided an exciting platform to bring young people together, the lessons in self-expression and group communication are the lasting aspects of a decade of involvement in experiential education. It had a profound impact on my life and my desired career.

Being an outdoor facilitator is gratifying, and a whole lot of fun, but it is also seasonal and doesn't pay too well. As I reached my mid-twenties, I left the outdoors school world and ventured into creating new year-round businesses focused on human potential.

Fast-forward a few years and I was operating a small leadership development and consulting company focused on event facilitation and workshop development and delivery. I won a contract with a health organization that gave me the audacious and slightly uncomfortable title of Community Development Leader. In this initiative I was tasked broadly with increasing the health of young people in the Cariboo and Chilcotin regions of British Columbia by finding places to invest small amounts of capital which could have a large impact. Key to the success of this initiative was leading conversations to learn what people felt would inspire increased health based on their local knowledge. This was meant to be a grassroots initiative; in my region it focused both on First Nation communities and small municipalities.

As part of the process of distributing funds I facilitated a number of conversation-based meetings to decide how to do this in the most impactful way. I soon became painfully aware of individuals and organizations with vested interests who dominated agendas with their personal mandates. Academically, I understood interest groups and mandates, but experience is the very best teacher. These people and groups arrived at planning meetings with the pre-established goal of securing additional dollars for their existing projects. To be sure, many others arrived simply to learn, to join the conversation, and try to facilitate a group outcome. Unfortunately, those people were in the minority.

I wanted to involve everyone in a real conversation, and not just provide a platform for the loudest voices. So, I had to innovate.

Along my educational journey as a group facilitator, I came across a game called "35." It was exactly the tool I needed in this situation. The idea was simple: To learn what a group values, you ask an open question and give everyone a recipe card or sticky note to write down their answer. A common question was: "What is the most important thing we need to talk about today?" Each person wrote their answer down and did not sign their name. The cards were then shuffled around the room by people exchanging them with one another, one at a time, until they were told to stop. Each person then looked at their card and rated the idea out of seven. This shuffling and rating happened five times. At the end of this ordered chaos, I collected the cards and counted backwards from 35 to find the highest-rated cards. The agenda was then formed based on the top-rated items.

By adding this structure to a conversation, everyone who came to the event had a chance to contribute their thinking and for their thoughts to be validated and evaluated. This transparent process revealed what mattered to the group. People with special interests couldn't disproportionately affect the event by hijacking the agenda or overwhelming the conversation. Everyone felt included in the process because it was deemed "fair."

This consistently successful activity fascinated me: It became the first step along a path of learning how to scale conversations. Inside this little game were critical components which could be examined and then scaled up. Practically, it boils down to four things you need to provide everyone with:

1. A safe place for diverse people to share independent thoughts

2. A bias-free method for everyone to evaluate thoughts one by one

3. A fair process for all thoughts to be evaluated equally

4. A method to understand what thoughts matter most

Along with my initial experiences gathering perspectives in my role as a Community Development Leader, I was hired to facilitate an assortment of events, with 50 to 100 people, in which a mixed group of stakeholders, with different needs and agendas, needed to agree actions. While tackling subjects such as local economic development, policy, strategic plans, health spending, etc., I constantly leveraged the conversation power of the facilitation tool "35." It consistently created great insight and the necessary buy-in for whatever actions resulted from the gathering.

This was my foundational experience of scaling conversations: Anyone can repeat it at a face-to-face event with a stack of recipe cards and a pen for everyone. I recommend changing one aspect of the instructions you can find online: Instead of having pairs of people debate the cards and agree how to distribute points, simply instruct everyone to rate their thoughts on a scale of one to five based on how strongly they agree (one = strongly disagree and five = strongly agree). This maintains the feeling of safety for the participants (the first hierarchy level of scaling conversations) and leads to a better group answer.

Moving scaled conversation into an online environment may have seemed like a natural progression to some, but it wasn't to me. I wasn't a "software sort of guy" and strongly believed in the power of being in the room with other humans; to look one another in the eye as ideas about the future were discussed. But my friend Lee White, former Executive Director of Outward Bound BC, observed "35" in action. He told me that a connection of his, Jim Firstbrook, had recently read James Surowiecki's *The Wisdom of Crowds*. Jim and his software development team had taken an angel investment from their former boss Amos Michelson, CEO of a BC company called CREO. They were apparently trying to build crowd wisdom software by aggregating ratings on electronic sticky notes in a similar way to my facilitation process.

I was skeptical, to say the least. But Lee was persuasive and resolute that there was power in the idea. He convinced me we should meet with Jim to share ideas at his upcoming launch event.

I learned later from Jim that, when Lee saw this potential, at the same time he had reached out to me he had also contacted Jim about this guy who drives around running meetings in remote communities using recipe cards. And Jim's reaction? Skepticism. Doesn't seem like a fit.

Fortunately, Lee succeeded in convincing both Jim and I to meet, and a few weeks later Lee and I traveled to Vancouver to attend the crowd wisdom software beta launch workshop. The rest, I suppose, is history.

After seeing this early attempt to facilitate conversations online I very literally dropped what I was doing and started working for the company, Thoughtstream, for free and for no equity. We had a simple agreement—to split the revenue from any early sales I could make as the beta product developed. I instantly both loved and hated what the team had built as their first guess at how to scale conversations online. But, one thing was clear to me: I felt passionate, and I wanted in.

The point of this is not what I did, but rather why. I had refined my face-to-face facilitation skills for nearly 15 years and had experience with many different methodologies beyond "35," including well-known gathering formats, such as World Cafe and Open Space. I was proud of my skill and my growing reputation but I was also growing increasingly disappointed by the limitations of face-to-face events.

Attendance at collaborative planning events was typically poor. Many of the people who did attend had good intentions but were also privileged and homogenous. Methodologies like the "35" game prevented or stymied big personalities and extroverts from taking over any agenda. But the results of employing "35" were ultimately still dictated by the people in the room. The staggering majority of people ultimately affected by the decisions of the small group were not able to be in the room. Every facilitator I knew was trying to attract more people, larger groups, to their events to avoid small loud groups taking over agendas about decisions that affected a lot of people. This same problem exists in nearly every organization in the world. Millions of people affected by decisions about training, funding, strategy, etc., have no, or very limited, ability to be a part of the conversation about those decisions. Much to the detriment of the outcomes.

The internet held amazing promise. Jim and the team had a huge idea. With the right structure anyone can go online to participate and share their diverse and independent thoughts, in any time zone, and even in any language. Algorithms can ensure all thoughts are seen by everyone. Digital "sticky notes," and the thoughts on them, can be translated into any language in real time, and shared with people worldwide in a microsecond. The wisdom of the crowd can be leveraged to solve nearly any challenge an organization might face. While not everybody has perfect access to the internet, the number of people who do completely dwarfs those who can equitably participate in face-to-face conversations about issues that affect them.

A few years after Lee and I met with Jim and saw the beta software, we passed over a million people exchanging thoughts on our newly named platform: ThoughtExchange. We provided a platform for hundreds and even thousands to come together and share their voice to tackle all kinds of problems. I worked with a superintendent in a school district with 30,000 students. While hosting an online conversation on our platform the district officials had surfaced concerns and priorities from nearly 5,000 people. But in one school, in an extremely economically challenged neighborhood in the district, they only heard from about 30 parents. That particular school had hundreds of students, and therefore hundreds of parents. So, maybe 10% of people joined the conversation making decisions about their kids. Not so great, you might think. But here's the thing. I asked the superintendent: How many people from that school historically show up at town hall meetings or parent events? The answer: Between zero and four. But usually, unfortunately, zero. The school tries their best, but no one comes. So, a group of 30 people sharing their ideas sounds pretty good. Those same 30 people, gathered in a virtual room, would be quite a force for change if you could access all of their diverse and independent thoughts: With that amount of support, you have the ability to incrementally improve. At zero you don't. Even with the best facilitator on the planet.

The reason I devoted the last decade of my professional, and much of my personal, life to this software company, and eventually became the CEO, was not because of a newfound passion for software and solving technical problems. Luckily, we have other people in the company who have that. My passion has always been for facilitating ways to draw forth the voices of as many people as possible and to leverage that potential. And the internet is the way to do that. It's more inclusive, more equitable...and safer than any face-to-face meeting.

With our new digital working environments—rapidly transformed during the early days of the COVID-19 pandemic—every organization now has a unique opportunity to leverage the benefit of internet communication to scale conversations. It was a huge change for me, going from a face-to-face facilitator, an experiential mountain guide, a workshop creator, into an enabler of internet communication. I missed, and to some degree still miss, the energy of the room and the personalities of the people who would show up, however privileged and homogenous. But to deliver on the mission of bringing many voices to decisions there is only one choice that scales. The internet.

After the murder of George Floyd by police officer Derek Chauvin in Minneapolis, Minnesota, people around the world protested to elevate the need to overcome the issues of systemic racism, police violence against Black people, and ultimately to ensure Black Lives Matter. Understanding their responsibility to be an ally and to participate in the dialogue, leaders from across many sectors held special events and scaled conversations on the ThoughtExchange platform. They asked questions such as: What can we do to improve our ability to be an anti-racist organization and to ensure Black Lives Matter? How can we better support our Black team members? What can our organization do to overcome systemic racism and discrimination? What is on our hearts and minds as we work together to ensure Black Lives Matter? Thousands and thousands of people shared thoughts and considered the thinking of one another as their organizations promised action and deepened their commitment to overcoming racism against Black and BIPOC people. One CEO described the impact of learning from his Black employees as the most effective day of learning so far in his lifetime.

As the CEO of a company that helped these leaders scale conversations with this gravity, I didn't (and still don't) feel satisfied with these achievements: I feel an increased sense of urgency. Hundreds of thousands of people participated in scaled conversations about the health and safety of students, teachers and staff in the pandemic, but millions of other parents did not. Hundreds of leaders scaled conversations to accelerate efforts to overcome racism, and yet hundreds of thousands of leaders did not. Anti-racism, global pandemics, climate action, LGBTQ rights, gun violence, remote worker mental health .... All of these are issues that require people to join the conversation. Now. It's not a matter of if they join the conversation, it's a matter of how.

More than the narrow goal of growing ThoughtExchange, with this book my hope is to do my part in moving forward a body of work that inspires more research, development, and deployment of conversation technologies to bring people together to solve the most pressing issues in our organizations and on our planet, before we become so divided we blow ourselves up or become so selfish we wreck the planet. With all due respect to those who are working to ensure we can leave the planet and inhabit airless, oceanless worlds ... my thinking is we should prioritize efforts down here on this world. It seems worth saving.

The same mechanism that helps revenue leaders increase sales helps public leaders save lives. It's about scaling conversations.

scaling

conversations

PART I

WHAT'S IN A CONVERSATION?

B efore I dive into how to effectively leverage our collective conversation strengths and overcome challenges to scale conversations to include hundreds and thousands of people, I'll first explore the components that are required to make a simple conversation successful with a small group—believe it or not, it can be summed up by one thing: Margaritas. After that I will cover the value of scaling that ability. Then, before discussing how to scale a conversation up I will address the attempts leaders make to include voices now and explain why they are typically unsuccessful. This is done through the lens of what people require to successfully converse.

CHAPTER 1

What's a Conversation?

MARGARITA THOUGHTS

A waiter asks a group what they'd all like to drink. First person answers: A beer. Next person: Sure, me too: a beer. Next few people follow suit and order a few more beers. One person orders a glass of wine.

Then, the final person says to the waiter: "A friend of mine said you make one of the best margaritas in town... and since it's the first hot day of summer, I'll take one of those."

Everyone else at the table considers this critical new information.

Then the first person says: "If it's not too much trouble, I'd like to change my order. I'd also like one of those famed margaritas."

Second person: "Me too."

Third: "Yep, me too, and unless I'm mistaken, make it a pitcher so we can just do a round of margaritas?"

The wine-ordering person is the only holdout. "I'll stick with my wine," they say.

This type of interaction is at the core of human communication. We share ideas, listen to one another, change our minds at the drop of a hat, and ultimately forget which idea belonged to who in the first place.

"I'm glad I thought to order margaritas!"

"That wasn't your idea, that was mine..."

"Was it?"

In any conversation with fewer than 10 people, this is, in a word, natural. Small meetings create dialogue and interesting solutions surface. A single idea can become the most important idea in a heartbeat. During small focus groups, or in small chats online, discussions take place and people change their views, combine thoughts, explore where there is consensus, and where there isn't. No problem.

But as soon as that group gets larger than 10 what happens? The most frequent thoughts are mistaken as the most important ones. In the margarita example, the waiter would never be able to discover the "margarita" thought with a large group of tens or hundreds, even if they used the highest standard of survey or polling technology. Every survey output, word cloud generator, person paid to codify feedback, and advanced natural language processing algorithm that clusters similar thoughts would do the same thing: Inaccurately emphasize that BEER! and words similar to beer are by far the best and most loved simply because that term was most frequently shared as a "first-thought-best-thought." When, of course, given the chance to participate in a conversation and consider the thinking of other people, no one in the group above even ordered a beer.

The curious thing about "margarita thoughts" is that, in a small group, this phenomenon of surfacing important ideas, instead of counting the frequent ones, is just so obvious.

Picture any meeting or group discussion you've had with six or seven people. As you try to solve a problem, everyone shares ideas as others react. Eventually, someone shares a thought that many people resonate with and that becomes an important thought that guides the actions you all take together. This is an extremely common and standard way of people working together. It's a conversation.

Now picture, in that same meeting, someone was listening to the conversation and counting the frequency of ideas shared. After the group arrives at agreement to take an action, that person interrupts and says: "Sorry, we can't go with that idea. It was only shared once by Julie and there are several other ideas that were shared more often early in the conversation. We need to use one of those earlier, frequent ideas. They are more important." That is obviously ridiculous. No one would do it. But maybe they would. And more importantly, maybe you would. In fact, you probably do. I'll explain.

Mistaking frequent thoughts for important thoughts is how most organizations inform decisions affecting many people. The annual survey run through HR is now a staple of almost every organization in almost every sector. These surveys are supplemented by special issue surveys/polls/pulses on topics such as Diversity and Inclusion, Culture and Professional Development. Some organizations even "pulse" weekly to measure everyone. During this now familiar process, a quantitative survey of questionable scientific value is sent to a few hundred or a few thousand people and the results are, let's be honest, hard to interpret. And for good reason.

I recall speaking with one leader who had the opportunity to talk with an employee who had anonymously provided an extremely low mark on their internal NPS survey. The question was phrased something like this: On a scale of one (low) to ten (high) how likely are you to recommend our organization to a friend or colleague as a great place to work? The employee gave an extremely low rating. Fortunately, they spoke up as the results were discussed by the team. "I gave that a one because all of my colleagues already work here and none of my friends work in our industry." They had interpreted the question as asking whether their friends would be suitable employees, not as a measure of their happiness.

In another, very similar scenario, a parent came forward after participating in a school district survey, which had asked a similar question: On a scale of one (low) to ten (high) how likely are you to recommend our school district to your friends and family? They had also given a rating of one. Their explanation: All of my local friends already attend this school district and my family lives out of town.

Ah.

"But how do you feel about our school district?"

"Me? I love it!"

It's worth repeating: Closed-ended responses are hard to interpret. To remedy this, along with the closed-ended questions most or all surveys now have at least a few open-ended questions asking for more context and explanation. In an effort to unpack various high and low marks in their surveys, leaders look to these open-ended responses for context. Modern survey platforms even help disseminate these open-ended comments by sending pages and pages of open-ended thoughts to managers and leaders in the areas of business related to the feedback. Facing this firehose of feedback, much of it directly contradictory, what do we do? Count responses. Theme them by frequency. Put them in word clouds to see which ideas are most...Common. The more frequent, the bigger they are in the cloud and the more influence the idea has.

If those people were all in the same room, you would instinctively know better than to count the number of times something was said. You would be far more interested in how things resonated with people, how they learned and changed their thinking after being exposed to the thinking of one another. You'd be interested in what emerges in a conversation as the most important ideas, which people agree on, and you would take note of the areas where people don't agree.

In early spring 2020, education leaders in the city of New Britain, Connecticut, were conducting a review of their curriculum, just as the COVID-19 pandemic was gaining momentum. Jonathan Costa, Assistant Executive Director of EdAdvance, a Regional Educational Service Center, wanted to scale a conversation and get the district faculty's thoughts and feedback on their return to school in the fall so his team could better respond to their needs.

"I was thinking we were going to get some instructional guidance," Costa shared with our ThoughtExchange team. However, as he quickly discovered, "If you don't feel safe, you're not going to be thinking about building a good lesson plan."

When Costa saw the trending thoughts in the conversation with approximately 800 people, it was clear that curriculum instruction wasn't what they were looking for. "I could *feel* the intensity of everyone's personal concerns for health and safety—their inability to imagine how we could safely bring people back to school without a guaranteed vaccine or therapy."

The surprising results from that online conversation gained the attention of Dr. Miguel Cardona, Commissioner of Education for the State of Connecticut. He chose to further scale the conversation about safety and the return to school amidst the pandemic to include the voices of teachers and parents across the state. Over a weekend more than 40,000 people joined a conversation where thoughts were considered by one another more than a million times. Ultimately, the Connecticut Governor, Ned Lamont, utilized the voice of tens of thousands to inform critical decisions that literally affected the lives (and, sadly, deaths) of many Connecticut residents. Schools were closed for the remainder of the year.

So, if your organization still counts responses from open-ended surveys, analyzes text, and mistakes frequency for importance, or if you start a conversation expecting it to be about one thing and find it ends up being about something completely different, your organization has something to learn from the lonely and powerful margarita.

CHAPTER 2

Why Do We Need to Scale Conversations?

Why do you need to scale conversations? I don't exactly know. Only you do. I know why I need to scale conversations. Everyone has their own problems, which they are trying to solve to achieve their own goals and aspirations; and, importantly, their own set of stakeholders, who expect to exercise their right to have their voice heard and who are affected by the decisions you make. You likely have employees, customers or community members affected by the decisions you make. Maybe you have all three. And, while I don't know why you personally need to scale conversations, I can help you discover why.

The key to understanding the "Why" is thinking in terms of capital. Capital is defined as the assets you have available for your purposes. Often narrowly defined as money, it's important to understand other forms of capital that are equally, if not more, important than the mighty dollar. To get at these, let's consider a term that in 2020 was used an unprecedented number of times, even more than the term unprecedented.... That word is crisis.

CRISIS

Crisis simply means a time of intense difficulty. All our communities, businesses, and personal lives contain crises. The real question about crisis is not if one will happen, but rather when one will happen next, and how soon will the one after it follow on its heels.

The year I write this book, 2020, has been a whirlwind of crisis. In a matter of months, the world has suffered more than a million deaths attributed to the Coronavirus. Economies are extremely uncertain. Racial tensions are increasing. Futures of all sorts are unknown. If there is one thing we can agree on globally, it's that we are experiencing crises.

We humans are resilient, however, and the good news is that you have survived 100% of your worst days so far. Not only survived, in many cases you've grown, learned, adapted, and even thrived. Crisis inspires change, and often for the better. As a result of the global unification around the issue of ensuring Black Lives Matter, billions of dollars (an estimated $7 billion at the time of writing) have been pledged by corporations to attempt to make irreversible and sustainable change in the areas of racism and discrimination. Trillions of dollars have been allocated in relief from the global pandemic. Businesses around the world have embraced remote communication and pivoted to survive, and sometimes even flourish, in this new world where people are more remotely connected than ever before.

Crisis, even more than necessity, is the true mother of invention.

And crisis contains an interesting element. One we need to focus on and leverage if we are going to succeed as a species on this planet.

A crisis arrives and causes pain. A solution is created and we experience joy. But something bad occurs with that solution and we're back in the pit of crisis. Then we react again and things seem to be fixed and happy. But then another, unrelated, crisis occurs. Damn. So, we make a big change and the change is good. But the change also causes a different kind of crisis and we need to regroup, adjust, and relaunch. This process is best visualized as hills and valleys:

CRISIS CYCLE

Crisis after crisis is one way to perceive our organizations, our society, and ultimately our lives. And if we left it there, it paints a pretty dismal picture. Crises after crises occur until a final crisis occurs and it's all over. But there's more. And there is hope. Crisis, like all things in the universe that have a position different from the norm, contains potential energy. That potential is growth and connection. I'll explain both.

GROWTH

First let's talk about growth. The good news about crisis is that, in retrospect, it is easy to look back at your life and realize that the crises you faced and came through successfully were necessary for your own invention and reinvention. Each challenge created a chance for learning and for opening your heart and mind. Taking that opportunity is what got you through and gave you perspective and increased your resilience. So, rather than simply waves of good and bad that ultimately end bad, instead these peaks and valleys are the materials that allow you to learn and grow. With the right focus on personal development, crisis can ultimately look like this:

CRISIS CYCLE

Growth is important for us humans, and as leaders, and while I don't want to minimize the negative impacts of crisis situations, many of which are caused intentionally by other people, I do want to emphasize the necessity and power of learning from constant adversity. The biggest problem with this concept is this: Crises are really hard. That's why they're called crises. And we need help to make it through and turn them into opportunities. Navigating them is really a team sport. That's why we need to discuss connection.

CONNECTION

Picture a leader or a mentor you have a very strong relationship with. Someone you would now do anything to help if you knew they were in trouble. With them in your mind, now picture those hills and valleys of crisis. Each crisis in your organization and in your life has a valley when it was extremely hard. After that valley comes a time of solutions and changes, which often also has a lot of joy associated with them. When in those hills and valleys do you think of that person you are picturing? Are they only in your mind at the top of the hill? During the innovation and solutions and changes and joy? Probably not. Probably that person you pictured is there with you in the valleys as you went through hard times, as you learned hard lessons, as you grew as a leader. They were with you through thick and thin, as it were.

Even more than being with you as you grew as a leader, that person you chose is probably someone who was more than that. They were probably an important, maybe even critical, component of your learning and success. Great leaders and mentors are people you have conversations with, and you share where you are stuck, and they listen deeply and share their stories and perspective with you. They help you navigate and thrive through crisis. And the more challenges you navigate with them, the stronger your connection with them becomes. The opportunities for connection with leaders during such crises looks like this:

CRISIS CYCLE

Navigating constant crisis creates constant opportunity to create connection.

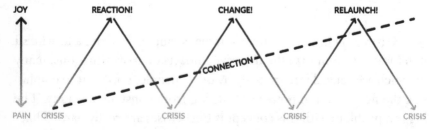

So now let's turn the table around. You are a leader with stakeholders. You have crises. Sometimes you have a whole lot of them.

The people you lead have fears and concerns and challenges they need to transform into growth and opportunity. And the more crisis you discuss with them—the conversations you scale—that you help them navigate, the more opportunity you have for connection. And the reward for this connection is capital.

CAPITAL

Capital, again, is defined as the assets you have available for your purpose: There are many more forms of capital other than money. And just like a bank machine you need to put capital in the machine first so it's there for you when you need to withdraw. Capital isn't a magic thing you create alone using strong words about your mission and vision. Capital is earned. So, let's discuss three forms of capital you need to earn as a leader: Relationship, Process and Ownership. Then I'll discuss how conversation can help you attain your goals.

Relationship Capital

Relationship capital is best described as: Be *that* friend. The capital you gain from relationships can be generated by being agenda-free.

Picture looking at your phone and seeing that a friend is calling you. Without picking up the phone you know, beyond a shadow of a doubt, they want something from you. Otherwise, they'd never call. We all have that friend, colleague or family member. Or maybe we are that friend. Who knows?

Now picture the last time you went out for lunch with a friend and you raced to buy them lunch before they bought it for you. When you see their number come up on your phone you want to make sure you aren't distracted when you pick it up because you're eager to speak with them.

The difference between those two people is relationship capital. One of those people has no capital in your bank and the other one does.

The critical question is: What sort of actions and events filled their account? What sorts of things did they do and say to build up capital with you in a way that others have not? The answer to this question will be different for everyone but will also contain commonality. The people who we have relationship capital with reach out when they wonder if they can help, not only when they need help. They ask what is in your heart and on your mind when they suspect you are struggling. They share in good times without requiring all of the attention being focused on them. Most critically, they know how to listen openly.

The next question comes after you reflect on the sorts of things that put capital in your bank for other people: How can this time of unprecedented crisis be a catalyst for unprecedented creation of relationship capital in your organization? How can you be that leader? I'm soon going to dive into how to scale conversations and, before I do, I want to explore first the benefit of scaled conversations in terms of relationship capital.

There are questions leaders have asked handfuls, hundreds and even thousands of people amidst the coronavirus pandemic to help increase authentic relationship capital:

> What challenges are you experiencing?
> If remote work continues next year, what concerns do you have?
> What hopes and concerns do you have about our future?
> What is on your mind right now?

These questions scale perfectly from a one-on-one conversation to conversations with thousands as everyone shares their concerns, challenges and thoughts. The asker ensures they do the most important thing: Listen. Following listening may come actions, but listening needs to come first.

The idea that leaders need to scale their most simple relationship-building questions is disarmingly simple, and I'll explore how to ensure entire organizations can feel heard and respected thanks to leaders asking the most simple questions. And the leader's role, that of actively listening to the answers people give about how they are feeling creates process capital.

Process Capital

Process capital is best summed up in the phrase "Never about me without me." This capital is what can be generated when leaders include people who are affected by decisions in the decision process, fairly and transparently. Much has been written about fair process and a quick search can find articles on sites such as the Harvard Business Review talking about the components and benefits. Here is how I have synthesized the studies and suggestions as they relate to scaling conversations.

The idea of fair process breaks into two concepts. The core idea of "never about me without me" is that, as intelligent humans, people prefer to be listened to when decisions are made about them. Simple. When that is accomplished, capital is generated. Even when leaders make mistakes with a change or decision, the fact that they showed people they respected them and listened to their ideas goes a long way to keeping people motivated and connected to the organization.

The second concept of fair process is that people will support and prefer the outcomes of decisions with better process, even with worse outcomes in some cases. Research on this topic has uncovered some extreme examples where participants in study groups were found to prefer worse decisions that had a good process than better decisions with a poor process. I think of this as the "tasty bad dinner" phenomenon. The essence is, people will be happier in a worse restaurant with worse food, and the food will even taste better, if they felt the decision to go to that particular restaurant was fair. By contrast, people will find a reason to complain about excellent food in a fantastic restaurant if they don't like how they were forced to go there. We humans value fair process deeply.

The underpinning of all of this is trust. People don't need to have things go 100% their way and they understand decisions are complex and leaders can't make everyone happy. Rather than hope for their ideas to be explicitly heard and actioned, more importantly people just want to ensure leaders are educating themselves as much as possible, and listening to the voices of the people affected, before making decisions that will impact them.

Once the process of how leaders maximize voice in decision-making is well understood by everyone, process capital is created. People believe in leaders who demonstrate fair process and who listen at scale. They will get behind decisions made by leaders whose process they can understand and they believe in.

To get at this on a personal level, ask yourself: Who are the leaders you trust most? What do you believe to be true about how they make decisions? I believe you find them to be open to learning and known for being so.

Here are some questions leaders have asked on scale to show fair process as they work to address emergent challenges as rapidly as possible while ensuring as many people as possible are onboard:

What can we do as an organization to better support our Black team members?
What are your concerns, thoughts and questions as we make plans for re-opening?
What does leadership need to consider as we work through this transformation?
What are your thoughts or questions on the new comp plan?

In each of these question examples, changes need to be made that affect people on a very deep level and the first step is to be curious with as many people as possible to show fair process in decision making. McKinsey partners Andrea Alexander, Aaron De Smet and Leigh Weiss wrote about this in 2020 in their article "Decision Making in Uncertain Times." They highlighted the importance of including as many people as possible to ensure fast and successful decisions. The challenge of course is: How?

The good news about process capital is that it is plentiful during a crisis. The more we experience change in our organizations, the more we have the chance to increase process capital by asking people for their voice, not their vote, in decisions that affect them.

Ownership Capital: Don't engage, unify

Ownership capital is best understood by considering the difference between engaging and unifying. This type of capital is generated by providing people with as much agency as possible, aka freedom of choice, despite structures of influence such as perceived seniority, gender, ethnicity, ability, etc.

The difference between engaging and unifying is important. The idea that leadership needs to "engage" people has within it a core assumption that the people they are engaging, aren't. Put yourself in the shoes of someone who a leader is trying to "engage" with. How does it feel to be told you are being offered an opportunity to "engage" with your place of work? Or that you need to be more "engaged" with your child's education? Or thanks to a communication initiative you now have a chance to "engage" with your community? I'll venture that it feels belittling and a little patronizing. Most people I know already feel pretty engaged in their day-to-day work, engaged with their children and with their community. Their leadership are more likely to be the ones who are out of touch and not engaged. While it is admirable for a leader to be motivated to more deeply engage people to increase their feeling of ownership and agency in their organization, it is helpful to adjust the intention as well as the language to: Unification.

Great leaders understand that, rather than engage the disengaged, their job is to unify the existing intelligence, passion, and efforts of their people with the most effective direction of the organization. Rather than engage people with surveys and focus groups to attempt to achieve ownership, it is more effective to remove the assumption of disengagement and work to unify their intelligence and effort with yours by asking for their voice in ownership decisions.

It is also important to recognize that ownership is not limited to material things. It can apply to ideas, missions, visions, etc. Of course, it does apply to material things as well. People feel very strongly about their budgets, their physical environment, their benefits, their compensation, etc.

Creating ownership capital can be achieved by sharing challenges with people and asking for advice. Notice I said advice, not feedback or input. Advice is something you ask for from people you trust. Feedback is something you ask for from people who you are trying to engage. It may sound like semantics, but words matter.

Here are some questions leaders have asked to earn ownership capital. Notice they are asking for people's voices in decisions that materially affect them while not creating a false sense of democracy, or a sense of abdicating leadership. (I'll cover this in detail in a later chapter.)

As we plan the upcoming budget, what advice do you have?
What are the most important resources you need to be successful?
What cost-saving options could we consider as an organization right now?
What are your thoughts and questions about the two facility improvement scenarios we shared?

In each of these questions, leaders are making expensive decisions, sometimes in the hundreds of thousands of dollars and sometimes in the hundreds of millions, and they are asking for advice from people close to the challenges. The questions themselves imply ownership: This is *our* money, we need to do our best with it; What are *your* priorities, thoughts, questions, and ideas? We'll do our best to listen to as many of the top ideas as possible. Simple.

With so many budgets changing and decisions being made in the new remote economy, there is enormous opportunity to create more ownership capital to bring people together as hard decisions are made. Scaling conversations sends the message that we're in this together.

Creating relationship, process and ownership capital creates the environment your organization needs to move forward. It is the not-so-magic ingredient that unlocks discretionary effort, improves culture, builds support for decisions and even passes elections. Now all you need to do is have those conversations. With everyone. As often as possible. It's not complicated, it's complex. Not an airplane, just a simple problem with many moving parts.

Let's dig into how to do that.

WHY ELSE ARE MARGARITAS IMPORTANT?

In the first chapter, I presented the example of the margaritas as a way to show how thoughts and ideas can be brought to light in a group setting. Along with surfacing the best ideas instead of common ones, there's another reason margaritas are important. And that lies in the process of surfacing them.

At the core of every human are two competing needs. The first is to be heard. The next is to learn. Starting at a very young age people want to be heard and understood, even when they can't find the right words. (Ask my mom; apparently, I had many passionate opinions both spoken and unspoken.) More than a desire or an instinct, being free to express yourself is a globally recognized right foundational to democracy, which speaks a little to its importance in each of us. When that right is taken away, as it often is by consciously and unconsciously biased leaders and systems, protests eventually erupt, either on a small scale in an office setting, or on the global stage, as we witnessed following the murder of George Floyd on May 25, 2020. Voices need to be heard, and the systemic racism that has resulted in the killing of so many members of the Black community is one of the most powerful examples of an issue affecting everyone globally, in which our individual and collective right to have our voices heard is critical and needs to be upheld globally so we can move forward as humans.

Sitting right next to this need and right to voice our ideas is the core desire to learn, expand perspectives, and discard tired ideas.

People famously don't quit jobs, they leave managers. I've interviewed and hired quite a number of people over the last ten years and inevitably during the interview process I attempt to look them deeply in the eye while I ask them why they want to leave their current role. What do they say most often? That they weren't paid enough? No. They weren't listened to? Nope. The most common reason is that they stopped learning. Stopped growing. The job became repetitive and their manager was in the way of them progressing and evolving. People need to move forward. And that process of moving forward requires discovering new ideas and discarding old ones.

Hanging in the balance between the two opposing forces of voice and learning is the essence of a conversation. Too much time sharing your own voice and not listening and learning from others leaves you feeling, paradoxically, unheard. Too much time spent listening and learning without responding and sharing your perspective leaves you feeling unvalued. The right mix of sharing and learning, however, creates conversation. And not just any conversation. A mutually beneficial and productive conversation. One that surfaces insight and builds belonging as a foundation for unified action.

To satisfy both the need to share new ideas and discard old ones in equal measure requires four simple criteria: openness, voice, listening and empathy, and shared understanding. These are the building blocks of the basic unit of a successful conversation. And while those criteria at first glance may seem simple, there is much that goes into each. After we understand all the components of the unit, we can dig into how to scale.

CHAPTER 3

Components of a Conversation

W hat constitutes a conversation? Certainly, we've all had countless conversations in our lives. You may well have had a dozen
or more today alone. Or have you? A conversation is more than
just sharing information or informing another person or group of
people of a decision. A true conversation is a dialogue that employs
openness, voice, listening and empathy, and shared understanding. To
understand the value of a conversation—and a scaled conversation in
particular—it's important to understand each component. Let me start
with openness.

OPENNESS

To enter into a conversation that has the power to create trust, the
first key element is openness. Everyone involved needs to feel everyone
else is open and learning. If the conversation becomes a loud someone
trying to convince you and everyone else of something they are dead
set on, that can never be characterized as a conversation. That's more
likely to be called a sales pitch, a rant, or worse, a lecture. But as soon
as it's obvious everyone is willing and able to learn from one another,
everyone will call that a conversation or a discussion.

So, what makes a conversation open? Many people think the way
to ensure it is open is to begin with an open-ended question. While
that's true to a degree, there is another order of openness that is more
important to start with: Intention.

Intention

Why are we having this conversation in the first place? What do we want to get out of it? What decisions might result? How urgent are the actions associated with whatever we'll be discussing? What are we not open to changing? Sharing intention creates the environment for a conversation to begin in a place of clarity. And clarity is kindness.

After you've established an intention, the second order of openness is also important: Holding space.

Holding Space

Holding space is one of the most underrated leadership skills. Many leaders expand to fill space with their voice and call it assertiveness. The opposite of filling all space with yourself is learning how to hold space for a group. Importantly, holding space doesn't mean talking for a long time and then asking: "Any questions? No? Ok, moving on."

Holding space takes skill. It creates a place where both sharing your voice and learning from others can happen. Leaders who are excellent at it are nearly invisible as they do it. The group interacts with one another and the leader artfully guides the interaction. Their skill is made obvious by the depth of the contribution of the group resulting in deep insights for everyone.

Leaders who are terrible at holding space are painfully visible. They say things like: "Anyone want to chime in or are you all just hoping we'll move through this quickly?" Or: "We're running a bit behind schedule but if you have a comment or question let me know and I'll try to address it." Such questions and comments as those ensure the opposite of space is created. Their lack of skill is made obvious as fatigue sets in and people feel the need to multitask in a collaborative setting. Leaders unskilled in holding space attribute the fatigue to food or time of day or stress levels but ultimately the responsibility for the space the group is in belongs to them. How many conferences and meetings have you been to where the speaker or facilitator fights yawns with PowerPoint?

The skill of holding space applies in a one-on-one conversation or a conversation with hundreds. The bigger the group, the harder it is to hold space for everyone, but the same concepts apply. First, you create an invitation for people to speak candidly and then you ensure they are heard. Simple right? Well... kinda.

The sorts of comments a skilled leader makes that create space for a group are:

"I'm curious if you will agree or disagree with what I am about to say..."

"As we go through this I'd like to hear from a few different people."

"Let's ensure we hear from people we haven't heard from in a while."

The key to holding space is to be able to ask the group for participation in a similar manner to the phrases above and to then ensure more than one person takes you up on your invitation as you get into a conversation that is defined using words like "we" and "us."

In ThoughtExchange, when we have more than 100 people together, whether face-to-face or online, most leaders attempt to hold space to allow anyone to take the mic (face-to-face) or unmute and turn their camera on (online) to speak after a presentation. To highlight the tension and value of the moment we call these people: Brave souls. As in: "Can we please have a brave soul share what they are thinking for the benefit of the whole group?" Or after a breakout session we might ask: "Can we get a few brave souls to summarize what you discussed in your group?" That kind of language acknowledges the fact that speaking in front of large groups isn't something to be taken lightly. We also wait a disproportionate amount of time to ensure someone takes the leader up on the request to speak. Once one person speaks you are likely to get ten other people offering to go next. We also acknowledge people who speak first regardless of what they say so it's obvious we encourage people to take a risk to speak in front of the group.

Holding space live, face-to-face or online, isn't a skill you can acquire overnight but it is definitely one you can continually improve on by associating yourself with people who are excellent at it and by being as curious as possible when someone successfully achieves large group interaction. How did they do that? What language did they use? How long did it take for someone to respond? (Twice as long as you'd guess!) How much framing was necessary to ensure people actually interacted with the speaker? (Also, twice as much as you'd guess.) There's power in silence, in giving people the chance to reflect and respond.

Holding space digitally is a little easier as it can be pre-designed and artfully communicated using writing, images, and video. You can take time to ensure you get it right and you can provide a high-level summary for those who only need that, and a deeper dive with relevant data for people who prefer to dig deep before they participate. You can provide graphics for visual learners, audio for audio learners and written numbers and language for people who prefer to read. Effectively, you can meet everyone where they are at. Digitally, you also don't need to get it perfectly right as you can even iterate and change as you get feedback, unlike the one-shot opportunity you have live. Finally, holding space digitally for participation can also be provided for people to interact with when it makes sense for them. Maybe in the evening in their pajamas when the kids are in bed. Maybe on their phone on the bus.

Once you set intention and hold some space, the next element to openness is, at last, the excellent open-ended question. I have an entire chapter on this later in the book. It is essential to get open-ended questions right, yet they only succeed in an open and safe environment where people are in the right space to answer them.

Consider a few different waiters.

Waiter 1: "What would you like?"
Response: "I'm not sure yet, I think we need some time with the menus and we probably want a drink first."

Waiter 1: "That's what I meant. But sure, I'll be back in a few minutes."

Waiter 2: While everyone gets settled, I'd love to get you started with some drinks. (Intention: Check!) We have all sorts of drinks, alcoholic and non-alcoholic, and if you have a particular need and don't see something on the menu, just ask and I'll see what I can do! Sound good? (Holding space: Check!) Who wants to go first with their drink order and set the tone? (Open-ended question: Check!)

Servant leadership at its finest.

Imperative to creating openness in a conversation is to set the tone through voice. Without a measured and deliberate voice, the likelihood of achieving openness may be diminished.

VOICE

After openness, the next element of a conversation is voice. Being talked at is not a conversation. This is a pretty simple concept, yet surprisingly overlooked in a majority of group interactions. How many meetings have a moment when someone asks "Any thoughts? No? OK then . . . moving on."

Being pestered by the resident extrovert is not a conversation. For a conversation to be effective you need to actually participate to feel you've had the chance to share your thinking and, while you did so, someone was actively listening.

Much has been written about collaborative/principled negotiation, with terms like "BATNA" and "being hard on the problem, not the people." If you are interested in exploring such types of negotiation, I recommend books such as *Getting to Yes* and *Never Split the Difference*. Despite discrepancies in the art of arriving at win-win solutions, where all parties remain in good standing with one another after the negotiation, all have a common element: The need for people to have the space to share their voice while the other party is actively listening.

Ensuring people have a voice in a conversation is mostly about structure. One on one it's as simple as letting the other person know you want to hear them out and then, in your own words, reflecting back what they said so they feel heard. It's a simple concept, but it's not easy to execute. In fact, in conversations with any gravity, this is far from easy. Yet, deep down everyone knows the right thing to do and can learn how to apply the idea in harder conversations with a little practice.

In a small group, it's about circles. The physical structure of a circle when face-to-face, and the process of a circle when online can have a transformative effect on a group.

During a ThoughtExchange sales kickoff offsite event in early 2020 I came into a room where our team was having a...spirited...discussion about some changes to structure and compensation. Our CRO Jayme Smithers was at the front of the room and 30 people or so sat in an assortment of disorganized chairs. As I stood at the side of the room and watched the group, I noticed things were a little tense. A few people were asking questions with a slightly exasperated tone, others were facing away from the group and others sat looking quizzical. When people noticed me, I walked up beside Jayme and saw a mixture of embarrassment and frustration on everyone's faces. This was a group in the classic "storming" phase, made famous by Bruce Tuckman in 1965. Tuckman asserted that groups go through four phases of development: Forming, Storming, Norming, Performing. The Storming phase occurs when trust has increased and people begin to share their voice more confidently...and often, more sharply. This can result in tension and frustration. The way to get through that phase, into Norming (and ultimately Performing) is to emphasize "tolerance" of each team member and their differences.

We like to frame all sorts of things as adventures in Thought-Exchange and Jayme, to his credit, immediately smiled with humility and said to me and the whole group: "Hey tail guide! I could use a bit of help here."

I made a joke about hiking and finding their group stuck arguing in a rainstorm and I said: "Let's get these chairs in a circle, shall we?" We needed to establish a structure for tolerance of varied opinions. A circle of chairs represents that well.

The group let out a sort of collective sigh of relief and everyone rearranged their chairs into a circle. Someone passed out sparkling water pretending to be a high-end waiter. As soon as the group was in a circle the anxiety reduced a fair bit and all I said was: "Let's go around the circle one time and ensure everyone can say what they need to say."

From that moment forward the conversation became productive as each person aired their perspective while everyone listened. By the time we made it around the circle, which didn't take all that long, it seemed apparent that all problems were solvable and, while we wouldn't make perfect decisions, we'd try our best to make the best ones for everyone. The circle was the most important element.

This simple act of placing people in a circle when things need to be said, again not easy but simple, was something I witnessed in the practice of Chief Mike Archie of the Canim Lake Band. I admired how people left his events feeling heard and closer together, even though not every problem was solved. I asked him what his secret was to make sure every event ended well. He answered, in his classically soft-spoken Mike Archie voice: "You put on an event and at the end you get everyone to stand in a circle and you ask them to say whatever they need to say for the event to be good. Then everyone says what they need to say. Then the event is good." Extremely simple and extremely powerful. Everyone has the right to voice their thoughts. If they don't exercise that right, it's their choice. Once everyone has been heard the event can be over. 100 people at the event? The circle is big enough for 100.

Those who know me professionally know of my admiration (read: obsession) for circles and for the people and cultures who understand their worth in building communities that respect and trust one another. Providing the opportunity for everyone to share their voice has the double benefit of uncovering all of the best thinking while also increasing belonging. What organization in the world doesn't want better ideas and more belonging?

During small online meetings physical circles aren't possible but what is possible is creating the essence of a circle. During our online senior management meetings where everyone is remote, we have a practice of hearing from everyone in attendance by selecting one person to begin and then asking that person to then select the next person to speak. And so on until everyone is heard.

All too often the excuse for not creating space to hear from everyone is time. Not enough time. Too much information to share, presentations to give, and updates to be provided to hear from everyone. It's a systemic problem that needs to be challenged if you want to recognize the benefits of hearing from everyone. When ThoughtExchange gathers 150 people together face-to-face, we don't close the event with a keynote, we close with a circle. It takes about an hour. It's funny to me how many ways we would prioritize an hour over the important act of allowing everyone to be heard.

With technology you can hear from thousands of people in less than five minutes. Yet the notion "we don't have time" to hear the voice of everyone prevails in many organizations. Which is why we need to learn how to scale. So it makes sense that listening and empathy are the next crucial components of a conversation.

LISTENING AND ATTEMPTED EMPATHY

After voice comes listening and at least an attempt at empathy. I group these ideas together intentionally to distinguish between the scientific description of listening from the deeper distinction of the listener being open to being affected. True empathy is the ability to share the feelings of another person. While listening with empathy is a gift, it is also tricky to meaningfully replicate in any conversation as we are all somewhat gated by our life experience. Anyone who has lost a significant person in their life can understand the difference between attempting to empathize with grief and empathizing with grief.

Before you have actually lost someone, the empathy is somewhat academic. But you tried, that's important.

The key concept here is to remember conversations require at least an attempt at empathy to succeed. The listener needs to be in a curious state as free from conscious and unconscious bias as possible for the speaker to feel heard. A great way to practice this is to actively work on staying curious by forcing yourself to ask open-ended questions as you listen. Questions such as these go a long way to keeping yourself in a curious state and the speaker feeling the conversation has mutual value:

And why is that important to you?
Can you help me understand that better?
Or, more bravely:
I can tell you have something important to say but I am having a hard time understanding for some reason. That is likely all my fault...

In small groups the ability for everyone to "listen" often relies on a leader or facilitator asking clarifying questions on behalf of the whole group to keep people empathizing as best as possible. In Thought-Exchange we talk a lot about "generous curiosity," which is a reminder for people to treat each other generously when there is a lack of clarity, and to approach misunderstandings with as much curiosity as possible.

Asking yourself "How can I be more curious in this moment?" can be a powerful catalyst to ensure listening happens.

The most powerful force preventing consistent listening and empathy is, of course, bias. The ability for people to be heard is limited by the ability of the group to hear through their myriad of potential conscious and unconscious biases; including, racial, gender, authority, professional credentials, cultural fit, age, experience, and on and on.

Bias training and conversations can help small groups improve their ability to listen and empathize. In large groups, I believe biases of all types need to be augmented by technology for people to feel heard at scale. This is an important topic and I will talk in much more detail about it in the next chapter.

The fourth and final component of conversation is shared understanding. In many ways this aspect closes the circle on the criteria of a conversation—creating a natural conclusion to what transpired.

SHARED UNDERSTANDING

Effective conversations need closure. Often, the need for closure incorrectly drives a need for resolution through stated "actions" or "outcomes." This is great in conversations meant to arrive at such things, but even conversations with no actions require an outcome.

How many meetings have you been in that result in a list of to-dos that everyone knows won't be done? The process of making a list removes the anxiety that a conversation was potentially a waste of time. Which is good. On the other hand, too many abandoned to-do lists create distrust.

Rather than engaging in only conversations that need to end in actions, it's better to ensure they end in shared understanding. The shared understanding may or may not include actions and this should have been clearly communicated at the beginning.

A famous concept in mediation is: When in doubt, summarize. That is to say, if you get to a place where a conversation stalls, provide a summary of what you've heard and what you've said and see if that creates an opening to move forward.

The same rule applies at the end of a conversation in a small group. Summarizing the thoughts that resonated with the group and outlining any actions, agreements, disagreements and areas for continued discussion is a great way to provide the closure that is in itself an opening to a future conversation. Even if the only outcome of a conversation is a better understanding of how and why people disagree, a summary of this increase in knowledge can bring the group together and create insight.

In small groups, asking various members of the group to summarize what has transpired, and asking for brave souls to add their voice to anything missing, is a powerful way to end a conversation.

In large groups you need a way to show people what was discussed, what resonated, and what did not at scale.

With a clear understanding of what a conversation entails, and earlier reviewing why it is important to scale conversations, you may be ready to jump in and start bringing the conversations you have to scale. Not so fast. Scaling conversations is simple but it is not easy—either for the individual leading the conversation or the people who are part of the conversation. It is a new process for everyone to learn and trust and adding many voices also adds many opportunities for mistakes. Let's explore why conversations are so hard to scale.

CHAPTER 4

Why Are Conversations Hard to Scale in Person?

The components of a successful conversation are readily available and relatively easy to understand and put into practice. Be open, ensure everyone has a voice, encourage listening and curiosity, and summarize shared understandings. We all get it wrong much of the time but we can all try our best to improve in each of those areas, making our group conversations increasingly effective.

If I never had to scale conversations to include more and more people, this book would be complete. And also, perhaps devoid of any useful insight.

Nearly every organization, at some point or another, needs to create capital by gathering insight and creating a sense of belonging with more people than can fit around a table. Larger group conversations are attempted yet they fail to create insight and belonging in both obvious and hidden ways.

The most obvious ways things fall apart, within small and large in-person conversations, is social awkwardness, loud voices, and biases.

SOCIAL AWKWARDNESS

Groups of 15 people don't sit around and discuss topics of importance, in much the same way a table of 20 probably doesn't discuss drink options—they just order. And "beer," aka shallow first-thought-best-thought, wins the day. Groups larger than about six people require a facilitator to keep the conversation inclusive and productive. No organization has an unlimited supply of expert meeting facilitators who can ensure large conversations include all voices and create the space to allow the adoption of unique perspectives by the group.

Why six people? Well, there are many theories but the simplest answer is time. With more than six, the general feeling is there isn't a structure to usefully hear from everyone. As a result, to avoid awkwardness the group admits defeat before the conversation starts. The only way to overcome this is by adding structures like facilitation, rules and timekeeping.

Loud Voices

How many group meetings have you attended where the leader, who likely thinks best by speaking out loud, thus subjecting everyone in the group to their thought process instead of working through silently, takes up 90% of the speaking time and one or two other people take up the remaining 10%, while a large group listens silently? That's a rhetorical question. That's most meetings.

This is such a common occurrence that it's accepted and expected even though people understand it to be a problem. Everyone knows the group can't take in, and get value from, everything the leader is saying. And everyone knows the loud voices that pretend to represent the larger group, don't. Yet it's accepted that a loud leader speaks and loud people respond.

The reason it's accepted is the interesting part. It comes down to a misconception of value. Leaders of conversations where only a few loud people are heard, value "informing people" and "being seen to be challenged" more than they value attaining insight and creating belonging. The perceived importance of people coming away from meetings feeling "informed" is paramount. After speaking for 50 minutes, and addressing questions from two loud people, a loud leader ends the meeting with one overwhelming feeling: Mission accomplished.

The same loud voices who spoke up in the meeting reach out afterward and confirm that the meeting was a success. So, the cycle continues.

This cycle perpetuates, not because those leaders are stupid, but because they are ignorant. In the literal definition of the word: Lacking awareness and understanding. The very first time a leader insists on a group circle, regardless of the time commitment, or leverages technology to hear from everyone immediately, is mind-expanding. It turns out the alleged quiet people are not quiet, and have things to say that are both helpful and surprising. And it turns out everyone is deeply grateful for the opportunity, and say so.

The solution to loud voices, the antithesis to their tyranny, is experience. And without knowing or recognizing there is a problem there is also no ability to transcend the reality you accept to be optimal. Experiencing the voice of everyone is something we will explore in depth.

BIAS

Even when expert attempts are made to hear from more than six people in a group setting, bias meddles. At its simplest core bias is an inclination for or against a person or group. This can be as innocent as unconsciously being biased toward the person who sits closest to you. At its ugliest, bias can consciously diminish any voice from a person of a different ethnicity or gender.

Regardless of intent—unconscious or malicious—the key to understanding biases is first to admit they exist. With that acknowledgment, the next step is to understand how to surface insight and belonging.

As with any behavior change, the catalyst for change is understanding what you lose if you don't change. Much of the writing you see in business magazines focuses on what is gained from being better humans and better leaders, with fewer unconscious biases. And while that's important, much writing misses the more important point that, with bias in conversation you are operating with fragile ideas and disheartened people. It's the classic vitamin vs painkiller argument. The reality of bias in group conversation is that it prevents critical ideas (margarita thoughts) from being discovered and makes people feel isolated.

Unfortunately, in every group there exists a complex web of biases that reduce the efficacy of a conversation. The problem they create increases dramatically as the group gets larger. More people bring more biases, for and against, while also adding their own unique brand of bias to the mix. The biases we bring can be grouped into three categories: Those you know you have, those you know you're unaware of, and those you don't know you don't know.

The Biases You Know (BYK)

Everyone has biases they are aware of. You probably know you tend to ask for advice from people who think and look most like you. You know you trust people with familiar or impressive credentials over people without them. You are more likely to listen to your longstanding connections vs your latest. Etc. These are the niggling bias moments you do your best to navigate and the list of biases you know grows over time as they get revealed to you. In any group conversation, everyone at the table has a list of biases they are aware of and, hopefully, they all do their best to overcome.

The Biases You Know You Don't Know (BYKYDK)

Everyone also has a list of biases they know they don't know. These are the sorts of biases that leaders can admit to having, even before they are able to completely understand and address them. Systemic racism is an example. More and more leaders admit to the reality of having racist bias they are working on uncovering and overcoming. They use phrases such as "inherited bias," or "systemic bias," to both admit it exists and to admit it has not been addressed. The bulk of effort in removing bias lives in the realm of transforming the BYKYDK into biases you are aware of and can at least manage.

This work is important and the list is unique to everyone. Cognitive bias, gender bias, racial bias, confirmation bias, credential bias, extroversion bias, and on and on.

Transforming the BYKYDK into BYK is significant and requires deep work.

The Biases You Don't Know You Don't Know and... You Don't Even Know You Don't Know Them

This is the last category of bias. If you want to explore a scary bias, google "parole granted after lunch".... The essence is that a study conducted by the Proceedings of the National Academy of Sciences found hungry judges grant fewer parole applications than nourished judges. Ouch. Hangry bias.

Within each of us is an enormous list of things we bias toward or against for reasons completely mysterious to us. The same way we prefer tastes and smells, we value particular ideas and people for reasons that seem to be genetically imprinted in a way we can never understand. It can only be described as a defining characteristic.

These kinds of biases are the hardest to see and the hardest to overcome. While it's possible to hate olives and then keep trying different olives in different forms until your tastes evolve and you end up loving olives... it's not an easy process. And not a common thing to undertake. People who don't like olives simply... don't like them. In the same way, we are predisposed to experience things that cause us happiness or pain because of events in our past that create pathways for chemicals to be released when certain experiences occur. Our unique life experiences and related chemistry make us seek out similar experiences and chemistry in ways that can be productive or counter-productive. Sometimes very counter-productive. Many biases are inherited and deep-seated, and so difficult to see that they run us and we don't realize it.

Examples of these sorts of nasty things are studies that show tall people are paid more. People with high cheekbones are treated more favorably. People with familiar names have different experiences to those with unfamiliar names, etc., etc. As you can well imagine, the list is long and getting longer.

In essence we have a conveyor belt of bias. At one end there are mysterious biases we try to transform into biases which we can at least name but can't successfully navigate. After we have named a bias, we seek to understand how to try to stop it from preventing insight and belonging.

I'm not a bias expert and I don't have expert advice for how you can manage the biases you and your team may have while you inter-act face-to-face in group meetings, etc. If bias training is new to you, there are many experts and resources to help you undertake the valu-able journey of reducing their negative effects.

The most important aspect of biases as they relate to scaling con-versations is: They are there, they are plentiful, they are cleverly hid-den, and they are getting in the way of uncovering actionable insight and creating belonging. Great ideas are not shared; or, when they are shared, they are not recognized. Diverse people don't contribute or are dismissed; when they are it leaves them feeling isolated. Those who see a bias which is not obvious to others feel frustrated. Those who feel they are themselves bias-free appear to others as ignorant and arrogant. And on and on. The reality of bias in large groups is that it's a mess.

And while I feel reducing bias in organizations is a critical activity, I also believe as you work to solve challenges in your organizations you can't wait for this education to fully succeed. It is a long process. That's an understatement. As a species we've been working to overcome biases which any rational person would see as completely insane, like assessing where to find intelligence based on skin pigment or gender; and we're only now considering all of the other bias that is running our lives and causing havoc.

While we improve on the individual level we urgently need to find ways to actively augment our bias with technology. Scaling con-versations effectively is impossible without the removal of as much bias as possible so ideas can be evaluated on their merit instead of the perceived merit of the people who share them. More on that in a later chapter.

Even if we can imagine a meeting with more than six people in which an expert facilitator ensures everyone is heard, and participants have been trained to recognize and reduce the impact of conscious and unconscious bias, we still have a problem when the group gets larger. In a word: Beer. Frequency is mistaken for importance.

BEER

Aggregation and prioritization of thoughts is a critical element of a conversation that creates understanding and action. As conversations scale up this becomes more challenging and quickly impossible. Simply hearing from 30 people where everyone has five minutes to speak their thoughts takes 2.5 hours, never mind the step of people agreeing or disagreeing with each individual's thoughts to learn what matters most and then arrive at an action.

Recognizing this analog limit, leaders of large group interactions resort to gathering thoughts on notepads and sticky notes, physical and digital, and allowing facilitators and consultants, with expensive top-shelf bias, to group and theme them. And invariably they highlight the ideas that are . . . mentioned most often? Frequency gets mistaken for importance. Ideas that would have been deprioritized in any small discussion instead get written down and evaluated by their commonness. Beer wins the day. And everyone can plainly see that it is not a powerful idea that represents them. Oh well.

Recognizing the lack of true insight and connection, leaders initiating large face-to-face discussions tend to limit their next discussions to smaller, more focused groups. Scaling conversations in an online environment has its own challenges. I dig into that in the next chapter.

CHAPTER 5

Why Are Conversations So Hard to Scale Online?

Prior to COVID-19, global organizations and remote companies were already experienced in online communication for all aspects of business. Post-COVID-19, the rest of the world caught up. Quick. As the pandemic took hold across the planet, anyone wishing to collaborate with groups was forced to do so with technology. Video meetings, messaging apps, online conferences, social media, surveys, e-learning, and all manner of group communications became the norm for every organization. Necessity is the mother of ~~invention~~ adoption. Companies providing online collaboration tools, such as Zoom, Slack, Microsoft Teams, and my company, ThoughtExchange, experienced an enormous increase in usage as leaders scrambled to find ways of bringing people together utilizing technology.

Whether organizations you are involved with have been conversing digitally for decades or only a single year, you have by now experienced all sorts of attempts at digital interactions to make up for the lack of face-to-face ones.

But more than just a replacement for a face-to-face interaction, the promise of online communication is enormous. Transcendent actually. The promise is far beyond the range of normal human experience. Software dramatically reduces, or removes, the limitations of space and time and cost; it allows any number of people to connect with each other's thinking instantly, in any language, in any location on the planet. It's both a painfully obvious truth and also a shockingly powerful capability that was hiding in plain sight.

The potential of online conversations inspires all kinds of attempts to allow people to connect with each other's thinking. These attempts at scaling conversations have many challenges we've all experienced. These are so significant that most people don't put much value on online dialogue.

How many video meetings have you left feeling less connected than when you started? How many work-related and social media group message threads have caused you to slap your forehead in a mix of disbelief and frustration?

Or asking the other way: How many online conversations with more than six people have you participated in where you felt you were heard, you learned from other people, you trusted the insights revealed, and you felt an increase in belonging?

Probably not many. And that's because online conversations face different challenges that get in the way of their success. Loud online voices, unheard voices, and crowd madness are some key challenges that prevent conversations from scaling well digitally.

LOUD ONLINE VOICES

Picture the family member, maybe a cousin or an in-law, who is the first to post dramatically and publicly on Facebook or Twitter when any-thing political happens. With that person in mind, ask yourself: Does this person represent your thinking and that of the majority of your family? I'm guessing the answer is, in a word: Nope.

But could other people who don't know you or your family all that well make an assumption that they represent your thinking, at least in part? Yep, I believe they could. And that's too bad.

But what do you do when you see or hear about that social media post your family member made that is not in alignment with your opin-ion? Do you respond on Facebook or Twitter publicly to set the record straight? Do you get the balanced majority of your family to opine on social media in order to create a more balanced dialogue? You probably do neither. You likely do nothing except maybe make a few comments verbally, not online, about the problems with social media and the disturbing fact that people might think your family member represents you when clearly they. do. not.

Like loud voices in a large in-person group setting, loud voices online tend to dominate and shut out others. Who wants to be attacked publicly on social media? Not you. Or me. So, an extremely small number of people who say things that do not represent the thinking of the larger group talk in an echo chamber on the internet where their ideas are served to their friends who are the people who have the highest chance in the world of adding a "like" or two. As a result, a controversial statement gets two likes and no pushback and it is considered online engagement.

There are all kinds of reasons why someone might be extroverted online, but delving too far into behavioral psychology about their motivation risks losing the key point: Just as loud people in face-to-face meetings suck all the air out of the room and get in the way of surfacing great ideas and creating belonging, in almost every digital attempt at a conversation there are loud voices who do the same thing.

And people who are the first to speak, but who don't represent the majority, exist in your email threads, your messaging apps and your video meeting chats. And, worst of all, they are probably your closest allies.

If you post an update on Slack, Microsoft Teams, live in Zoom or WebEx, on email, or however you communicate digitally as a group, notice who replies publicly. Consider that they don't represent everyone but most everyone else is too afraid to engage and appear to disagree for fear of a painfully visible public debate.

In your workplace the loud voices are not your relatives, at least not normally, but it is important to recognize they are there. How can I be so sure? I'll explain in a later chapter. But the essence is that experience is the best teacher. However painful. While the loud voices online are hard to ignore, the silent majority—the unheard voices—are the ones who need to be brought in to scale conversations effectively.

UNHEARD VOICES

The flip side of loud voices is the faces of the people who refuse to engage virtually. There are people who sit back and watch messaging threads and email chains and virtual meeting chats and effectively say nothing. Who is that person? Probably it's you. And me. And most people. In many or most online conversations it's just too painful to wade in with your thinking, especially if it is candid and contrary, for fear of derailing everything or creating a public fight of sorts.

So, in most online "conversations" you have a loud leader proclaiming something or other and a few reactive people responding while the majority watch with apathy. Apathy, not because they are cruel people or disinterested in their work or organization. They're apathetic because they can't imagine a better way. The current way of discussing an issue as a group is broken...but...I can't think of a better way, so let's just let the loud people chat online and I'll weigh in one-on-one with someone who can hopefully represent me. In the meantime, have at it loud people. I am going to sit silent with the unheard majority and we are all going to collectively sigh together as we watch the conversation carry on in a vacuum of misrepresentation and agreement.

Unheard voices are as much a problem as they are an untapped resource. They are the majority, and systems and processes to hear from them have near nuclear potential in terms of new, fresh and creative ideas and solutions.

The final reason scaling conversations online can be a challenge is because of crowd madness, or the idea that large groups flock together for irrational and unhelpful reasons.

CROWD MADNESS

I remember walking with my family on a beach with a mile-long stretch of hard sand between the shore and the water. Far far out where the sand finally met the water a small group of people were gathered. They were too far away to count accurately but over the course of a half an hour we saw the group grow in number. Maybe they had found whales? Seals? Sunken treasure? Who knows? We decided we should not miss out on whatever it was they were gathering to witness. So, we made the mile-long trek with our tiny kids out to the group. You probably guessed what we found there. A group of people! Everyone asking why everyone else was there. No one knew. They all came because they saw people who seemed to know something they didn't. No whales. No sunken treasure. Just 70 people in a group with more on the way.

I also remember talking to friends the days after the Vancouver B.C. Stanley Cup riots of 2011. After the Canucks lost to the Bruins thousands of people flipped cars and destroyed store windows following a hockey defeat. Millions of dollars of damage from looting and several people were injured. Many theories arose about who had instigated the riot. More interesting to me was learning that several friends who lived in downtown Vancouver had watched the game and the resulting riot coverage on TV and wandered over to check out the riot. Not to flip cars or loot. Just to witness it, moth-like.

Neither of these scenarios are organized protests or meaningful gatherings yet they caused people to herd together for illogical reasons. This irrational, mass gathering potential strikes fear into the hearts of many, or even most leaders, and for good reason. Crowd madness is a real thing.

Many online systems are set up exactly like the beach and the riot. They highlight a loud person or group and then gather people around them.

Take this study of Reddit on Max Woolfe's Blog called: **What Percent of the Top-Voted Comments in Reddit Threads Were Also First Comment?** He found the first comment submitted becomes the most upvoted parent comment a surprising 17% of the time; and, even more surprisingly, 77% of the time the top-rated comment was one of the first ten. Does that mean 77% of the time the most insightful comments are added first? Obviously not. It means a fast "loud" person is more visible and likely to attract a crowd.

The phenomenon above is now becoming a problem in nearly every organization, as messaging apps, with features to add votes and emojis to threaded comments similar to Reddit, are gaining market share and becoming standard communication tools. Even when comments aren't "upvoted" the reality is the first comments get the most attention and often discourage others from weighing in.

Nothing draws a crowd like a crowd.

With small groups of loud people dominating online channels and unheard people standing on the sidelines, except to come in occasionally as a crowd to upvote the fastest (not the most important) comments in threads, it is no wonder the majority of large communications are either one-way broadcasts or closed survey-like interactions. Critical structures like the talking stick, group facilitation techniques, and rules of order, that make small-group interactions possible, have never been digitized effectively. Without their influence, people behave poorly in large groups online.

Due to both conscious and unconscious reactions to the challenges created by this lack of structure, leaders who need to influence and gain insight from many people make mistakes they would never make with smaller groups. I'll outline those mistakes next and you can decide if you or your organization might be making some of them. After that we'll get to solutions to help address them.

CHAPTER 6

Typical Mistakes Leaders Make at Scale

The problems associated with scaling conversations online or face-to-face are real. And leaders know it. Instinctively, people know that well-intentioned conversations can quickly degenerate into a small loud group dominating with overemphasized optimism or pessimism.

You and I know this from experience. We've all witnessed a simple tweet or Facebook post that collapsed into an online knife fight. Some are the stuff of legend—internal posts creating havoc and amplifying the voice of the outspoken minority. Maybe you've heard a story of one simple negative comment about a company online turning into what looks like a free-for-all attack.

Whether because of direct experience or urban legend, leaders are wary, scared to open the floor to comment from a large audience for fear of creating the exact opposite effect they set out to create. They know that having a conversation at scale to show kindness and proactive leadership can accidentally turn into a rant session that creates division and dissent.

Without the right tools, these fears are correct and have been validated.

The real problem is not the challenges the above issues represent. The reality is the challenges are so great that attempts to include all voices in conversations are typically avoided at all costs. Though the number of leaders including everyone in scaled conversations is increasing, as digital tools like ThoughtExchange gain more traction, as of 2021, only a small percentage of organizations actively include diverse voices in decision making.

Canvassing ideas from large groups is further challenged by the inevitable mistakes leaders make in the ways they try to obtain that input. Creating space for scaled conversations takes time and practice. No one will get it right the first time...or the second, third or fourth time. Allowing people to be heard and to learn in an unbiased manner is a skill that must be nurtured. Instead, most leaders make some combination of these five mistakes:

Mistake 1: Manufacture consent with surveys

Mistake 2: Create division with surveys

Mistake 3: Invite thoughts into the void with Open-Ended Forms

Mistake 4: Rely on false representation with Focus Groups

Mistake 5: Politicize discourse with town hall meetings

Let me describe each of these mistakes in more detail.

SURVEYS: MANUFACTURING CONSENT

What is your favorite ice cream flavor? Wait, don't answer yet. Here are your choices. Pick one:

Licorice

Bubblegum

Chocolate Mint

How does that feel? Feels unfairly limited. Feels like I have an agenda to support three ice cream flavors and to disregard the rest. Feels deeply...uninteresting. Maybe even useless.

How about a political survey that asks what issue is most important to you?:

Carbon reduction

Affordable housing

Job creation

Other

Yuck. Even if they let me pick all, or none, or enter my own answer, I feel disappointed after almost every survey I've ever taken. Someone, somewhere, has an agenda and a reason for limiting my choices so they can make the masses feel they have given their consent to whichever falsely constrained selection, that are all deemed acceptable, is the most popular. What about systemic racism and freedom of speech? Can we agree those issues should be on the survey? Why not?

Noam Chomsky has written and spoken extensively about the deeper implications and drivers of manufacturing consent and how systemic biases function in mass media as a method of reducing democracy and maintaining control. This oversimplification is probably not something he'd endorse. In fact, I think any oversimplification is something he wouldn't endorse. But my use of the term "manufacturing consent" isn't meant for us to delve into political science. It's meant to serve a point: To attempt to gain buy-in and maintain control, leaders consciously and unconsciously gravitate to a strategy of only communicating certain information, limiting choice, and then asking people to rally around one of a few answers deemed to be acceptable by the leader in the first place. By its nature, this excludes all other input.

Ice cream and public surveys are easy targets options and are meant to put you at ease. What about the surveys you send in your organization? Who is in charge of deciding what choices are on it? Who designed the best practice? Why are some things off limits? What consent are you looking to manufacture as you do so? Your employees ask that question as they go through your culture and effectiveness surveys. Is it any wonder that you need to incentivize and inspire people to finish them? They aren't very inspiring to complete and, in turn, you learn very little from the results. Have you ever completed a survey and felt energized and that you learned a lot? Likely not, yet companies still send them out to gather voices on critical issues such as anti-racism and corporate culture, and organizational effectiveness. But the net result is apathy; perhaps, at best, a high five for trying. Thanks for coming out.

I remember a public leader describing the difference between a scaled digital conversation and a survey during a keynote. He said, "No one ever thanked me for sending them a survey." Surveys have their place but it's not to scale conversations. It's to measure and benchmark. Salary surveys to inform equitable pay are genius. Surveys which benchmark the gender diversity in your organization vs. other organizations with similar revenue, or in similar industries, are powerful. Surveys which seek to learn how your company culture can be better are less than ideal. Surveys designed to reveal concerns, and what your team needs to feel effective and empowered, won't work. Culture and needs assessments are conversations because you can't know what the answer is before you ask the question.

Nevertheless, "survey culture" thrives in nearly every organization around the world because it is better than nothing, and let's not forget that. Better than operating in a complete void is to know your leadership is at least attempting to unpack why your ratings on communication and culture have decreased over the last 18 months. It's better to understand that your sales team's satisfaction is decreasing than to not know.

But if you are a leader in those organizations, know also that we humans have developed a keen sense for identifying when our consent is being manufactured, consciously or unconsciously. As we sift through fake news and hone our understanding of the difference between misinformation and disinformation, we also develop a sixth sense for when leaders are unwilling to address subjects outside a predetermined mandate. Your people know that, instead of opening up conversations to discover areas of tension, ignorance and misunderstanding, your narrowly focused surveys are sent out with answers intentionally confined.

While, as a leader, you aspire to have your team feel you value them and their input, your surveys are likely to send a message that you are afraid of real discourse. The true result is the destruction of trust and motivation, despite the best intentions. Which leads me right into the second mistake leaders frequently make when trying to scale conversations: Unintentionally creating division and polarization through surveys.

SURVEYS: DIVISION AND POLARIZATION

I remember standing on stage in front of a large group of American school superintendents. "In a few moments, on the count of three, I am going to ask you to put up your hand with either one finger or two fingers raised," I told them. "If you believe schools need more weapons training and armed professionals on campus to decrease school violence, please put up a one. If you feel weapons don't belong in schools and need to be taken out of the hands of more people across the county to help decrease school violence, please put up a two."

Then I waited for a few long moments. "Do you have your number?" I asked. "Well don't worry, I won't make you do that. You can relax, I'm not going to count to three." The room let out a collective sigh. Some nervous laughs and some head shaking.

"Why was that a tense moment?" I asked them.

"Divisiveness," offered one superintendent.

"Emotionally charged issue," offered another.

"We don't agree," offered a third.

I agreed with all of them. I explained the reason I did that is so we could all experience the power and emotion of being unfairly divided into false groups. While everyone in the room had their own relationship and experiences of gun violence and school shootings, the idea of being coarsely and visibly grouped into one of two camps was extremely volatile. No one wanted to turn that collaborative event into a polarized spectacle.

Having led digital conversations on this topic I knew there was a lot of agreement on the need for schools to address mental health and inclusiveness through careful collaboration with psychological and enforcement professionals. I also knew that, when it comes to protecting innocent children, rural superintendents who have schools 45 minutes from a police station have different opinions than superintendents in urban settings, even when they have similar political leanings and live in the same state. So, the notion of asking them to put themselves into one of two pre-determined and unfair groups contained explosive potential.

In a similar vein, a public school district once sent out a poll to learn which school calendar was preferred by parents. Their intention was to gather feedback from and include parents in their decision process. In a district serving tens of thousands of students, hundreds of parents answered the poll. The results were about 55% for one option and 45% for the other. The leaders noticed it was a small group who answered the survey and took the lesson from the research project that the public was "on the fence" about the calendar preference, basically 50/50. The school district selected the option that, according to the survey, had 45% popularity and communicated that everyone was equally divided, so they had selected the one they felt worked best.

Can you guess the result? Was everyone happy the community had been included? Nope. The visible part was the protest that got local media attention. The less visible part was the volume of upset emails and phone calls the district received. A vote had been cast. The people had spoken. The leaders had denied and defied the democratic decision.

Of course, the school district leaders who devised the poll were shocked. This wasn't, in fact, ever meant to be a vote. The decision wasn't going to be made via referendum. The exercise was intended to include more people in the research to facilitate a good decision. And it backfired. Badly. It caused people to picket district offices with signs. The people who voted within the 55% approval scenario had expanded their membership.

In both of these scenarios, leaders put people in groups they weren't in a moment ago. There are no two clear camps on how to keep kids safe. There are no two ways to do a school calendar preferred by two explicit groups of people. There are nearly as many opinions as there are people involved in the survey. But, once assigned to those groups, pre-defined by the those who developed the survey, ownership of opinion grew and polarization mounted. Instead of participating in the empathy-building process of learning from collaborative discussions and seeking common ground, the mechanism of grouping people into buckets created strong emotion.

How might your surveys be doing the same thing? Questions as simple as asking people to rate their satisfaction around topics such as diversity or communication have the power to divide an organization. Though more subtle than the binary stories presented above, the act of consistently forcing people into boxes that don't quite fit can create ongoing emotional turmoil that is harmful to your organization. Picture all the questions in your culture surveys and consider the factions they represent if you made them put up their hand publicly to show their answers. Just because the answers in a survey are anonymous doesn't mean the polarization does not occur. Any mixed score on any survey question demonstrates the divide. The resulting harm is determined by the question that is asked and the way the results are actioned. When some leaders say things like: "I'm proud to share how much we have improved our rating around inclusiveness in the last six months," when the score has gone up from three out of five to 3.25 out of five, the reality is dissent and polarization.

By avoiding conversations about issues that matter, and forcing people into predetermined groups, it's interesting to ponder what emotion and reaction you may be unintentionally inspiring.

You might think, then, the narrowness of surveys with predetermined choices would be counterbalanced by a form with open-ended questions. Unfortunately, such open-ended forms are another mistake that leaders make when trying to scale conversations.

OPEN-ENDED FORMS: INVITE THOUGHTS INTO THE VOID

Knowing the limitations of closed-ended questions, many leaders nevertheless endorse sending out a limited number of wildly open-ended questions via online forms or short surveys, consisting mostly of a few text boxes.

I recently received one myself. A local organization wanted my input on four subjects. Four open-ended questions. Conceivably, sent to tens of thousands of people. Their intention was to show me they care about my voice. Their choice of communication tool inspired exactly the opposite reaction in me, and in others. People commented on social media, "Why are we not using a transparent and two-way platform?"

Maybe this mistake can be summed up by an iteration of an old favorite: "If 5,000 trees fall in the forest, and only one person is there to hear all of them, do they all really make a sound?"

Ok, maybe it can't be summed up via a remix of vague philosophy, but the essence of the tree-falling question is asking: What do we mean by sound? Sure, the airwaves move but, without a listener, is there a sound? (And yes, yes, let's leave the animals with ears out of this debate.)

When it comes to whether or not I feel heard via submitting a form, the answer is clearly, "No." How could I be heard? If thousands of people answer, how will they deal with all of the feedback? Is one person reading them all? And how can they decide what matters? Are they going to make a word cloud? Is a college student going to group and theme all of the answers? What happens then?

More than worrying about everyone sharing thousands of thoughts, my deeper concern is that the process seems futile to everyone; therefore, only a few people will share extreme thoughts and the results will not be representative.

I have no idea how many people will participate in this survey I've received or what they will say. The problem is the process itself is opaque and the results, whatever they might be, seem extremely hard to action. And even if they say they took weeks to read and prioritize actions related to the thousands of people who submitted ideas, it makes me wonder: Now, what are they going to do with all of that?

While almost everyone who has sent a survey that contains a few open-ended questions can agree the qualitative answers are the most valuable part of the undertaking, those same people agree the process of dealing with open-ended comments is completely overwhelming. With no sense of who agrees with what, thoughts are put into buckets and everyone attempts to find patterns and create summaries. Actioning anything, never mind everything, is extremely hard.

Instinctively, as people encounter a series of open-ended questions followed by text boxes, they know the process of listening and actioning results will be ineffective. SurveyMonkey alone has 60 million registered users. Just think of the vast number of open-ended questions created. Most leaders in most organizations have encountered open-ended survey results either personally or through an organization they are part of. Many people have experienced the challenge of dealing with open-ended text firsthand.

And, while the technology is improving to serve particular open-ended results to particular managers, and allowing machines to group similar thoughts together using algorithms that find similarities in words and sentences, even the result of a whole bunch of organized thoughts sent to various people is somehow uninspiring to the participant. Why? Because it still feels as though you are sending thoughts into a void and the leader doesn't much care about you.

As a customer you experience this all the time. You encounter the open-ended text box for feedback while you shop online or in your email after you buy a car. How was your experience? Rate it and then tell us how we can do better! When you read that, are you inspired their product team deeply wants to know what you think and how you can contribute to the success of their organization? Or does it feel like you'll be sending thoughts into a void?

What a leader wants is for it to feel like a conversation and a sign of respect. But, similar to qualitative surveys, results and intentions are not the same. Surveys and open-ended forms are ineffective and imperfect ways of gathering input from a large group. In-person gatherings—focus groups and town halls—have potential for eliciting valuable input, but leaders make many mistakes here too. Let me tackle focus groups first.

FOCUS GROUPS: RELY ON FALSE REPRESENTATION

At a core level, margarita thoughts are understood by everyone. Great ideas surface in great conversations. New ideas emerge through the process of learning from one another and prioritizing what matters most.

The problems with surveys and open-ended forms are understood enough that they are not relied on too heavily when true change is happening. To launch new products, integrate new cultures, fund large capital projects, etc., leaders know it is critical to get in a room and talk to people. Nothing compares to the experience of hearing people out, encountering what moves them, and basing decisions on the reactions of real live humans. Focus groups are the way to go then, right?

Unfortunately, focus groups aren't scalable. There is not enough time in the day, or beans in the budget, to move everyone affected by a decision to a location where they can all talk with each other. And, even if you had the time and money, deciding what mattered most to all of the focus groups would be impossible.

Instead of solving the scale problem, most organizations work to create focus groups that are representative. Representative of your customers, representative of your employees, representative of your community. That way you can get great ideas and show people your process, and they will feel you have included them via someone who represents them.

But all you have to do is describe your attempts to create a representative group to realize just how hard, even impossible, that really is.

In trying to embrace the diversity of the people you lead you quickly realize there are too many variables to transform focus groups into mini versions of your larger organization. Race, gender, seniority, authority, location, performance, politics, etc., etc., etc. The only way to assemble a group that represents everyone is to invite, well, everyone.

Various tactics are undertaken to determine "ideal" focus group participants. Things like:

1. Only invite top performers to sales focus groups. They sell the most anyhow so we most need to hear from them. But, why are the medium-performing people not doing as well as they could? Too bad we can't hear from them.

2. Only invite customers who fit the profile of the people who spend the most money with us to product focus groups. They matter the most. But why don't other people spend more with us?

3. Make the invitation open to everyone and see who attends. Put them into the most diverse groups possible. But then a very particular group shows up: Self-selected people with time on their hands. Do they represent everyone? Where are the single moms and busy managers?

4. Hire someone to figure out how to include the broadest possible representational groups. Wipe your hands of responsibility and rely on experts. When attendance is poor, or someone mentions they don't feel the groups represent your customers, employees, or community, point to the group you hired and have them reply. Doesn't sound so valiant, does it?

Focus groups and councils are common in many organizations, yet so many products, changes, and initiatives still flop. Diversity work is about discovering all the ways we are diverse and working to leverage them. Yet, using a small group to determine how everyone feels is the direct opposite of this. It suggests that individuals are so similar that people who look and act like them can represent them. How would you feel if your organization picked someone who looked like you to represent you in a big decision? You wouldn't like it. Not because using a representative group will probably be adequate and arrive at a correct answer. The truth is you feel left out. You wouldn't like it because you'd be pretty sure that, without your input they wouldn't arrive at an answer that is right and will work for you. It's flawed thinking.

Similar to surveys, discussing ideas with small groups of people is better than doing nothing. It's helpful to iterate products and ideas and ensure the creators aren't in a complete vacuum. The mistake is assuming you have everyone's perspective and claiming that a representative group of your peers was consulted and so, therefore, you should be happy and agree with whatever happens next.

Again, this is one of those obvious things from the participant's point of view, but leaders seem to dismiss how they themselves would feel if decisions were driven via representatives who were not them. Empathy is hard.

Town hall meetings are the other in-person setting which leaders like to convene to bring together a large group and attempt to share and receive ideas. But, as with focus groups, the settings for such meetings have their own pitfalls when it comes to scaling conversations.

TOWN HALLS: POLITICIZE LEADERSHIP

Have you watched a town hall with political leaders or candidates on TV, or on the internet? You know the ones. A few leaders sit awkwardly on oddly tall chairs and take pre-determined, "hard-hitting" questions from a panel of voters. It's hosted by a celebrity. It's recognized by many politicians and the media as international political best practice.

What is a word describing how you feel when you watch those events? Is it "trust"? No? Is it "connection"? Wrong again? How about "staged"? Maybe words like: "Political, sterile, biased . . . maybe even: a little bit desperate."

Why do those sorts of terms resonate? The intention of those events is to allow leaders to attempt to create increased connection with people, ultimately for their own gain. They need your vote so they can get ahead. These highly polished town halls are now amongst the more popular televised events during an election cycle, but they weren't always this way.

Town hall meetings, which don't usually take place in town halls, originated before the TV era as a way for politicians to meet face-to-face with their constituents to understand how they think and feel. The roots are deep in community-building best practice: You create an open forum to genuinely hear from the people you seek to represent. Town hall meetings are utilized by all sorts of politicians in many democratic countries to attempt to better understand their constituents.

Compellingly, they have been adopted by more and more leaders in non-politically focused organizations. As the importance of voice and representation to accelerate organizations becomes more evident, CEOs, D+I Leaders, VPs of all sorts, School Superintendents, etc., are hosting more and more "Virtual Town halls," where they speak to anyone and everyone who can attend. Some leaders during the onset of COVID-19 even did "daily town hall meetings" to keep everyone together. You probably do these or attend these in your organization.

Here's the thing. I am not so jaded as to assert leaders who attempt town hall sessions are only trying to win votes. Often, the motivations of leaders wishing to gather and hear from people are sincere. But adopting a model with its roots in politics has a consequence. Can you guess it? It's pretty easy to accidentally make things...political. The structure of these events often contains polished-looking leaders delivering polished information and navigating sterilized interactive portions of the show. Very similar to the televised versions we see. To increase "engagement" people add things like live polls and get people to group themselves in line with predetermined questions. Sometimes they host a live Q&A in which a slightly opaque process is used to submit questions that are sometimes upvoted by participants, Reddit-style. The software of those platforms ensures the safety of the leader so they don't get surprised. The larger the town hall event, the less truly interactive these things are. And as the people who produce these inter-actions well know, often a number of safe questions are "planted" so leaders can pre-prepare their answers.

As with all other forms intended to include multiple voices in decision making, town halls are better than no town halls. It's great to hear from leaders, they can be energizing and useful. But the meetings can feel staged and cold, and expand the gap between the leadership and the people they are meant to lead. Let's go back to the key components of a conversation, to gain insight and build trust: Openness, voice, listening and empathy, and shared understanding.... Most town halls have almost none of these things. They are mostly one-way, closed, and about informing people, not arriving at a shared understanding. Charismatic leaders can alienate themselves as they adopt political techniques for constituent input.

The good news is town hall meetings have the potential to be the most successful method available to you for genuinely conversing with everyone. People are gathered, leaders are ready, challenges are pressing. The only thing missing is the competency and technology to scale conversations.

The optimist in me wants to point out that all of the mistakes leaders make, as they attempt to scale conversations—from surveys and open-ended forms to focus groups and town halls, indicate we are moving in the right direction as a society. In every organization more leaders are gathering more people to understand more perspectives. Even when they get it wrong, by over-surveying or making things more one-way and political than they need to be...at least they are trying. I unequivocally believe getting it wrong is a critical step toward getting it right. So much of our history as humans is dominated by people with power making terrible decisions without considering the feedback of the people who will be affected by those decisions.

In the first part of this book, I explored the power and limitations of the mighty conversation. I shared the sorts of things that make conversations successful. I presented why we need to scale conversations and why that is hard to do.

In the second part, I'll look more closely at how to scale conversations effectively, focusing on the components of successful scaled conversations, what makes good questions to help scale conversations, and the power of including voices in the decision-making process.

PART II

HOW TO SCALE CONVERSATIONS EFFECTIVELY

For the last ten years my team and I have been iterating on how to scale conversation effectively with thousands of leaders and millions of participants while uncovering research to help refine and explain what we're learning. As I mentioned in the book's introduction, the core insight of the game "35" was the foundation for learning how to scale the essential elements of a conversation to include the voices of everyone while levering the wisdom of the crowd:

1. A safe place for diverse people to share independent thoughts

2. A bias-free method for everyone to evaluate thoughts one by one

3. A fair process for all thoughts to be evaluated equally

4. A method to understand what thoughts matter most

In Part II, I will explain and unpack each essential element. Then, I move on to consider the golden question: I know how to scale conversations, now, what questions should I ask? After consideration of who needs which questions asked and when, I'll address how to synthesize results. The book concludes by considering how to apply these ideas to create value by effectively tackling meaningful topics.

CHAPTER 7

Components of a Successful Scaled Conversation

A conversation, a successful conversation, doesn't just happen. To scale a conversation, you must create a safe place, the method you use needs to be bias-free, and there has to be a fair process for each thought to be considered. And you, as the conversation leader, must have the necessary tools to understand what matters most.

A SAFE PLACE TO SHARE INDEPENDENT THOUGHTS

This first element has two pieces that need to be explained one at a time: Safety and Independence.

Safety

Safety is defined as the condition of being protected. The learning here for scaled conversations is what people need to be protected from. When facilitating an event in which the agenda was set using the game "35" (described at the start of the book), I found that, when everyone was given the chance to share an agenda item from the safety of anonymity, everyone participated. Every time. This is a simple but powerful point. In a typical agenda-setting process for a large group conversation, those with privilege and power are typically the only ones to decide what the topics will be.

In soliciting ideas for setting the agenda, the next thing I witnessed was the power of a safe process. Since every participant had had the chance to contribute to the agenda, those same people mostly reported feeling the meeting was a productive use of their time. Similarly, they also reported feeling the outcome was acceptable because the process was safe for everyone, fair and understood. If you've attended any number of large group sessions, you can appreciate how rare it is to receive this kind of feedback. I've since found all sorts of research on fair process that verifies my experience, including the Harvard Business Review's articles "Fair Process: Managing in the Knowledge Economy," by W. Chan Kim and Renee Mauborgne, and "Why It's So Hard to Be Fair?" by Joel Brockner.

But, along with a broader notion of process, underneath all of this was the main principle that everyone in the room had the explicit opportunity to share their voice in a safe manner. Safe from bias: Their thoughts were rated without the rater having information about color of skin, gender, authority, professional affiliation, politics, perceived expertise, etc. Safe from privilege and power taking away their right to share their thoughts. Safe from interest groups drowning out the voices of individuals.

When ThoughtExchange first built technology to scale conversations, we had a platform where people would respond to an open-ended question and then react to the thoughts of others. Initially, we had names attached to each response and rating. As we asked questions about our company's development, we felt it was critical for people to understand who shared each thought and to know how various people rated each other's thoughts so we could take action. Radical transparency. Ultimate actionability. Or so we thought.

The same time we did this we also noted, compellingly, that very few people in our own small startup responded to invitations to join internal digital conversations on our own platform. We were small enough, about 30 people, that we made up all sorts of excuses about the "strength of our culture" and the "value we placed on candid one-on-one conversations that could never be replicated in larger organizations."

Our belief in the power of candid face-to-face (or video-to-video) conversations was so strong that we went quite a long time with names attached to all thoughts until someone on our team turned our organizational philosophy back on ourselves to challenge us to simply test our assumptions. We are fans of the Lean Startup and believe in the MVP culture: Test, fail fast and iterate. Someone said: "Well, instead of deciding on whether it is better or worse to remove names from thoughts and ratings, how about we just try it?"

So, we did.

The results were instantly impactful. Immediately after sending out a few questions when names were removed from the software, participation almost doubled. I wanted to know why. We were small enough that we could ask all sorts of people why they had participated in exchanges without their names attached.

The results surprised me.

"I don't want to be seen as the know-it-all when you ask questions to the whole company."
"I didn't participate before because I worried if my thought got rated high I would be seen as some sort of suck up."
"If my thought gets rated low, I'll feel stupid for sharing it."

"If I agree with the thought of a senior leader, I don't want people to think I'm being political when they look at the ratings."
"When people don't know it's me who shared a thought, I'm more interested in how they will rate it."

Notice that these responses are about slightly surprising flavors of safety. While I am sure it was also important for some to have their identity anonymized to share their candid thoughts on potentially divisive issues, people in general articulated a strong feeling they wanted people to be engaged with ideas, not personalities. Or, put another way, they wanted to be protected from bias.

At the heart of this is the key to any powerful communication process. Engage with ideas not people. Address bias. Great organizations should aspire to be idea meritocracies where the value of thoughts themselves over the many, many things that could bias other people while they consider the ideas.

The increase in participation alone would have been enough to convince me of the power of removing names from thoughts and ratings to increase safety. In addition to increased participation, I witnessed an increase in candor. Positive and negative. Results of exchanges contained a much broader spectrum of emotion and ideas as people felt free to share . . . well . . . freely. As CEO I still personally feel that freedom to this day. Inside an exchange, my thoughts are judged on their merit, not on my authority. I equally enjoy when my thoughts get rated high or low because the learning is free of bias so therefore much easier to accept. Whether people agree or not with my thought, I get time to reflect on the thought itself and that allows me to act accordingly. It feels like a superpower to know how people feel about how you think without also associating your thought with you. And I think this superpower is your ability to learn rapidly in a productive state of mind.

All of this learning initially took place inside our largely homogenous, high trust and very small company. Brought to the masses over the next decade this had a huge impact.

It turns out that, in all organizations, there is immense and largely untapped power in ensuring that people have the right to share their thoughts without fear of bias, discrimination, or retaliation. Participation is equitable. It's larger. It's more honest and helpful across the board. It gives voice to a typically unheard majority of people who want a platform to participate but don't have one. This allows leaders to make better decisions as they hear from more people, including those who have been traditionally ignored, or even suppressed, because there wasn't an appropriate platform for them.

What about trolls and disingenuous negativity? Well, it turns out that offering safety to everyone inspires the hearts and minds of the unheard majority we touched on earlier. These are largely the balanced people who want to help your organization succeed. Employees who choose to work for you, customers who choose to engage with you, and community members you work hard to serve for the most part are invested in helping you succeed. When you have an overwhelming response rate from so many people with helpful intentions, the tiny minority of destructive people get prioritized low or even moderated out by the group if their contributions are disrespectful. Just like a face-to-face roundtable, one or two unfair and negative people have a hard time taking over a conversation with active participation from many level-headed and invested people.

After millions of thoughts considered and rated hundreds of millions of times, I can say with confidence that safety is a critical element and the best way to achieve it is to disassociate identity from thoughts and reactions. And with safety ensured comes the independence of thoughts brought forward.

Independence

People are groupthink, crowd madness, bias machines. Countless studies—just google "problems with groupthink" and note the sheer volume of research and thought leadership in this area—have shown the problems associated with people being influenced by a group, and the group making terrible decisions despite the participation of highly intelligent people. The conclusion from most of these sources is that loud, influential people tend to lead perfectly smart people in some pretty dumb directions.

The value of independence is in direct opposition to groupthink. People are different. It's as simple as that. It's as simple as valuing that. They think differently and that's a good thing. People have unique knowledge and experience to draw from when they respond to an open-ended question and if you want to be effective, harvesting that uniqueness is absolutely critical. And the method for doing that is to present everyone with the same cold, hard, open-ended question and to get each person to respond without first reviewing the thoughts of everyone else.

To the person who responds, this can be intimidating at first. Am I taking this question in the right context? Is this what the leader was driving at by asking this question? Staring at a totally open question with no knowledge of how others have interpreted it is an interesting experience. And it is one that is completely necessary.

My first experience with this was in the earliest days of building ThoughtExchange. I used the platform, with our tiny team of ten or so, to ask how I can improve a job posting. It was one of my first experiences using the platform as a leader and, while the topic was not terribly compelling, the results were nothing less than completely fascinating.

The first response was the sort of thing I would expect:

"Could use more focus on communication skills."

The rest were not:

"There are extra spaces after periods in three different places and it's missing an apostrophe in the final sentence."
"The logo is the wrong resolution."
"That font won't show up well on our site and it is too long compared to other postings we are putting up."
"Is this the right timing for this position?"

I had to go back and look at the question I asked: "How can this job posting be improved?" Almost every person took the question to mean a different thing and each and every response made the posting better in ways that surprised me: Including questioning the impetus of the job posting itself. That tiny little experience cemented in me the power of independence. Chatting it over with people who had participated, several mentioned they weren't sure what I needed and looking at the responses of others they wondered what feedback was most important. As the person preparing the ad without an HR or marketing team to help, every single piece of feedback mattered.

A more recent example has more gravity but the same fundamentals. A few years ago, as ThoughtExchange was scaling and training our sales organization, we asked everyone in sales what they most needed to be their best and most successful selves. Some answers were what we expected:

"Top 5 ROI stories from our customers"
"A content management system for all of the collateral"

Others were less expected:

"Let us loose. I sometimes feel like even though we have permission to succeed, there's hesitation to let our team take risks and make mistakes."
"More opportunity to stretch my skill set and to operate more at the edge of innovation in my daily work without feeling like there are others always defining that for me."

Those last two thoughts were rated extremely high. They weren't training programs, software systems, mentoring programs. They were infinitely more important. Autonomy, trust, freedom for innovation. These are the sorts of things that humans require to be motivated and to be their best selves. Along with being powerful thoughts, they were also a real wakeup call. They inspired deeper conversations about personal development and performance and motivation that all tied into their success and therefore into the success of the company.

If we had sent out resources and had them select the most important or had them review our definition of resources and then contributed their own ideas on top, we would have achieved groupthink. More resources. But through independence, and thanks to the way a few people interpreted the question, we got to some bedrock that helped us accelerate sales performance in an unprecedented way. Independence matters.

The safe place to share thoughts independently is critical but only the starting place, not the end. A method free of bias is what makes a conversation a conversation.

A BIAS-FREE METHOD TO EVALUATE THOUGHTS ONE BY ONE

As I examined in the sections on margaritas, surveys, and open-ended text responses that escape into the void, simply asking for people's voice and calling it a day is not sufficient when your goal is surfacing revealing insight and building trust. No one feels heard unless they can clearly articulate the method by which the listener is listening. On the high level, the key to scaling a conversation is to ensure you are scaling both the opportunity for people to share their voice and scaling the system for those same people to consider the thoughts of other people who will be equally impacted by the decisions that result, and to indicate their overall level of agreement with those thoughts.

In my analog "35" activity, you can imagine the difference if I asked 100 people to write down their agenda ideas on a recipe card and then had them hand them in for me to simply read and then decide what we'd talk about. No, or far less, safety for anyone to independently share their ideas. Instead, the actual process of the activity includes the second step, where the facilitator asks everyone to consider the thoughts of one another as we shuffle the ideas around the room and everyone has the opportunity to score them based on how much they agree. This simple mechanism contains many important behavioral psychology elements that are critical to a conversation.

The first element is that each thought should be considered one at a time. Just as in a conversation where you can't hear two people talk at the same time, neither can you read more than one thought at the same time. The idea that everyone should read an entire page of thoughts and upvote only their favorite ones is similar to trying to listen to a group of people. At first you assume you'll read all thoughts and evaluate them equally but you soon find yourself gravitating to things that catch your eye. Overall, it's a terrible idea to create a system, whether online or face-to-face, where everyone is meant to consider large numbers of thoughts together. How am I so sure? Good judgment comes from experience. And experience? Well, that usually comes from the fallout of bad decisions. Yep, I've done them both.

The analog version of this mistake is a common facilitator practice that I used to do and I now actively advise against. The process is simple. Get people to share ideas on sticky notes and then hand them into the infinitely wise facilitator, me. Then I, and sage facilitators like me, group and theme the thoughts together before putting groups of thoughts on tables or up on walls. At this point we dole out a limited number of sticky dots and get people to indicate which groups of thoughts are most important. And that's where you have to be hyper-conscious of bias.

The grouping and theming step is the most explicit moment for bias to ruin each and every attempt at people considering and evaluating the thoughts of one another. To ensure the groupings are limited in a practical manner, we sage facilitators take some...liberties...as we put thoughts into neat broad categories. Only after our bias is thoroughly applied are people allowed to indicate their level of agreement with the new, higher level, themes. The most ego-centered facilitator will feel their grouping of thoughts has done nothing but add value to the thoughts themselves. Lord knows I felt this way: I have "sense-made" these thoughts into a digestible format. Participants are now welcome to participate at the highest level.

Having been a participant in this same process many times I know I have encountered the results of consultants doing their grouping/theming and I remember on several occasions sitting and looking at my poor thought in a group of similar-ish sounding thoughts and feeling this process now has pretty much exactly zero value. Simply, I felt unheard. I also began thinking about the rationale for the various groupings instead of considering each thought. In other words, preoccupied with the process, I didn't listen to others. It turns out the difference between the thoughts is more interesting than their similarity and I wanted to engage with the thoughts themselves, but I couldn't. They were locked away in safe groups. I wanted my thought to shine alone, but it couldn't do that.

Imagine this process in a conversation with eight or nine people and it's rather hilarious to picture. A leader in a small conference room asks the group a question and each person whispers their answer to the leader so quietly no one else can hear. The leader then ponders all of the thoughts, alone, and groups them into three high level themes. They then summarize the themes with pithy words or phrases. Finally, the group is asked to react to which theme they think is more important than the other two themes. Once the high-level theme is deemed the best, the leader thanks everyone and promises to "report back." This, of course, seems ridiculous. And if it is ridiculous for nine people, why is it sane for 90? Well, that's easy: It's not. I find this process of considering what a large group process would feel like with an individual or in a small group a very helpful sanity check.

That said, I facilitated many of these meetings and didn't arrive at the oddness of it through rigorous consideration. Only once I saw a better way did I understand the challenges with the first attempts. And, seeing the difference between sticky dot theme voting and the game "35" is only one of my educational opportunities. The first version of ThoughtExchange contained this same theming step. The first idea was to digitize the analog process in order to scale it. Sounds rational, right? Well on the positive side, it was more efficient to theme digital thoughts and create digital reports than summarize hundreds of sticky notes and to synthesize the meaning of sticky dots. But it wasn't long in the early days of the software before we realized we could digitally show everyone all the thoughts because effectively we had an unlimited amount of sticky dots and sticky notes in the software.

So, the next iteration of ThoughtExchange had participants viewing pages of unthemed thoughts and assigning a limited number of digital sticky dots to them. Nine thoughts to a page, 15 dots max. Sometimes we gave them ten dots; sometimes 20. We tried all kinds of dots. In facilitation this is force ranking by limiting the number of dots per thought. It was an interesting step in the right direction. But it had problems. Looking at a page of thoughts is hard. Comparing many thoughts to many other thoughts is also hard. In fact, it was so hard that users found it frustrating. Why 15 dots per page of thoughts? Why not 50? Or five? Good question. Why nine thoughts on a page—how about three? Or 15? Another good question. What is normal in a conversation?

By iterating and learning, iterating and learning we came to the radical, and in retrospect starkly obvious, idea that each thought should be considered one at a time. Just like a conversation. And, rather than force people to choose one thought over another, they could share how much they agree with each and every thought one at a time, just like a conversation. Also just like the game "35."

Through this process of learning and listening to people we reverse-engineered a very simple truth that was always in front of us. To scale a conversation from a small group to a large group you need to scale how everyone listens to and learns from one another in a way that actually works. One by one, with no identity, authority, ethnicity, gender, and sexual orientation attached.

With a bias-free environment for each person to consider each thought on its own merits, the next step is to ensure a fair process so that each thought can be considered equally.

A FAIR PROCESS FOR EACH THOUGHT TO BE CONSIDERED EQUALLY

The concept of a fair process for every person to consider each thought equally is extremely simple yet immensely valuable. Each thought needs an equal chance to shine. In a circle everyone has a chance to be heard. In the game "35" the mechanism is to ensure 100% of people write down one idea on one recipe card. In the shuffling step people simply wander around swapping cards with people until everyone has a new thought to consider. Each thought gets rated the same number of times. On the ThoughtExchange platform thoughts get served to other people as equally as mathematically possible to be considered and rated by other participants. When you do this trust in the process is established and you can get a great result. We considered all kinds of ways to attempt to improve the results by showing some thoughts more than others based on their content or who shared them. All of those ideas got thrown out because fundamentally they weren't fair, so they didn't work.

Many systems to hear from large groups allow for certain early thoughts to be seen and voted on more than other thoughts. Some systems elevate thoughts they turn out algorithmically to be more important. This not only introduces strange bias, it also creates distrust and creates bad results as early ideas aren't better than later ones. They are first. That's it. Do you want your thoughts to be heard equally? I do too. This section is straightforward and left intentionally short to make a point. Leaders should seek systems and processes that ensure voices are considered equitably whether it is in a small group in a circle, a large group using recipe cards, or online using technology.

With a fair process for people to express their thoughts safely and free from bias, the tools required to understand what matters most are key to the next step in the process.

TOOLS TO UNDERSTAND WHAT MATTERS MOST

In the game "35," with a relatively small group, it is easy to add up the scores written on all of the thoughts and see which ones mattered most to that group. Everyone can see and trust the process and the insights are obvious.

Once that scales up to more people than fit in a room you need more sophisticated tools. The margarita example falls apart quickly because of course when you talk to 500 people, you have more than one margarita thought. You have many thoughts people agree on. So, you need tools to break down the thoughts into groups without revealing the identity of the sharer. This can be done in a few ways.

The first is simple: To ask a survey question and then use the answer to segment thoughts afterwards. Asking 500 people a question and adding a survey response on where they live, for example, can get you information on what matters most to people who live in different locations. The survey question can be anything that breaks people into meaningful groups you want to understand more.

Another powerful tool to understand what matters to people is to examine rating patterns. By doing so, you discover groups of people who show they disagree by rating thoughts very differently to ultimately discover different thoughts they agree on. Think of this researching people about how they feel about strawberry ice cream. After finding some people who completely love strawberry ice cream and some people who hate it, you can then try to see if there is a common ground ice cream by attempting to find a flavor the lovers and haters of strawberry somewhat agree on. Maybe cookies and cream. With the results of digitally scaled conversations, you can find this sort of common ground between people who disagree about things by leveraging tools that seek out similarities and differences in ratings.

A final tool is to group or bucket thoughts together by whatever criteria you feel is important. You can group them by topic, urgency, clarity, etc. The key is doing this process after thoughts have been rated individually, instead of before they are rated (which introduces bias). This creates a way to disseminate insights to the comm.

The rapid dissemination of insight from scaled conversations is a critical aspect. Without it, a very large group of people feels "unheard" very fast. Conversations can't take months to understand and action. They need to be reacted to in days or weeks. Sometimes in minutes.

Much of the four steps I discussed above are focused and learned from in-person interactions, with some notes of translating it to online groups. But the challenge really, and our mission at Thought-Exchange, is to leverage the ability to scale conversation in online environments. That is where many conversations are migrating to now, even before the COVID-19 pandemic. Our businesses, industries and personal interactions are increasingly global. It's vital, then, that we have mechanisms to scale conversations effectively online.

CHAPTER 8

The Hierarchy
of Questions

A man walks into your office. He's visibly upset. You ask him to close the door and take a seat. He begins to speak and before he can get a word completed, you cut him off. "Before you say anything to me," you say, "I'd like you to start by telling me three things you most appreciate about our organization...and then...I want to hear one big idea to help us create a vision for the future we can strive for together."

It's a cringe-worthy scenario and everyone who reads it will say to themselves some version of: That's mildly comical—but—I'd never do that.

Are you sure you wouldn't? Maybe you already have many times. I'll explain.

In his research on the hierarchy of needs, and after connecting with Blackfoot leadership (please google this and then let's all give credit where credit is due), Abraham Maslow famously amplified wisdom on the reality that humans must have their basic needs addressed in order to attain the motivation to quest for the fulfillment of higher-level needs.

The first layer of Maslow's hierarchy begins with physiological needs, such as food and water and sleep. The next layer is safety and security related to health, property, employment. Above that is belonging and love, followed by esteem and accomplishment. After all of those needs have been addressed you can grapple with self-actualization and creativity. At the risk of oversimplifying a complex and academically debated subject, the basic idea is that it's hard to dream about the future when you don't know if you'll be getting a paycheck at the end of the month. It's hard to deepen relationships and lean into your creative genius when you don't feel a basic sense of safety at work. It's hard to celebrate what makes your culture strong when you are not sure how and when a new pandemic protocol might upend your team. It's hard to... these scenarios can be endless. But each time you address your lower-level need, a possibility opens up to explore something higher up the ladder.

Using that framework and applying it to organizational needs, in the context of question development, it looks something like this:

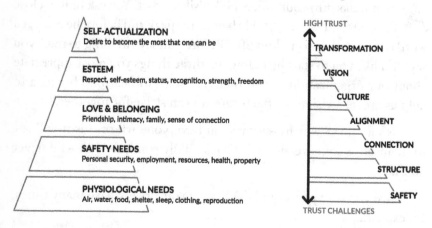

This hierarchy, when it comes to scaling conversations, is built in terms of teams and communities and contains the additional vector of trust. When trust is low you can't get people to truly embrace things further up the hierarchy. The only way to earn trust is by meeting people where they are at.

Though there is debate on the specifics and origins of Maslow's hierarchy theory, and how to usefully apply the concepts to educate and motivate people, there is a great deal of agreement around the core notion that a hierarchy does exist and should at least be considered in your personal and professional relationships. In any relationship you can easily relate to not being able to focus on achieving your potential when basic challenges exist around money or employment. And you can likely immediately bring to mind a moment when a basic physiological or safety need was met which inspired the exploration of love or creativity.

In small groups, most leaders are very attuned to this reality. In the example above, with the upset man, everyone knows the only thing to do when the visibly upset man walks into your office is to ask: "What's wrong?" Or: "How can I help?"

That one may be an oversimplification, but even a more complicated situation has a relatively easy answer in a small group. Consider a group of employees meeting for the first time after the company missed its sales targets. By a lot. Most (or at least many) leaders address the proverbial "elephant in the room" by stating the miss and outlying the immediate implications to the employment status of the people in the room. Instead, their need for security must be addressed before you can proceed with any discussion about changes or plans.

When that capability of earning trust through conversations becomes obvious to everyone, you realize the hierarchy-based thinking needs to become a cornerstone of your communication strategy. Assuming people are not upset and don't have basic challenges is a mistake that is easily remedied by remembering how to treat people in a small group. Said simply, ask them about their concerns and fears before you ask them to dream with you about the future.

As I explained in the chapter on mistakes leaders make at scale, the challenges of involving people in a scaled conversation about challenges using the wrong tech are very real. We know that. But once those structural challenges are addressed it's important to realize that you can communicate with hundreds or even thousands of people the same way you'd communicate with a group of five. You can meet entire communities where they are at as a group and find the common ground between them in order to earn trust and head up the hierarchy.

One final point on the hierarchy is the noted difference between Maslow's pyramid and the Blackfoot teachings. Maslow's pyramid has a focus on self with self-actualization as the top goal. The Blackfoot model has the focus on self as a problem state at the bottom of the pyramid. Only by achieving self-actualization can a person move up the hierarchy to begin to operate on the level of community involvement and then ultimately multigenerational transcendence for the benefit of all.

In the context of scaling conversations, the model is closer to the Blackfoot teachings than to the more popular hierarchy relating to the self.

The key to being able to drive your organization forward is to become a "hierarchy of needs" expert who can adapt to the current state of your people by asking them questions to meet them where they are at. This then opens the ability for you to ask the sorts of questions that will lead them beyond. Simple right? In theory, Yes, it's simple. Put into practice, it takes practice and time to get it right. To help you do that, I will focus on each of the seven levels of the trust hierarchy—safety, structure, connection, alignment, culture, vision, and transformation—and consider the sorts of questions that will help you scale the most important conversations in your organization at any moment.

Let's open each one up, starting with safety, which is the first level in creating the foundation of trust within your team.

Safety: How *Are* You?

Safety is the condition of being protected. When people lack this state they are likely to be living in their reptilian, survival brain that can cause any and all manner of fight, flight and freezing behavior. Many of us felt we lived in a lack of safety for most of 2020. The uncertainty about COVID-19 all around meant we all felt unsafe. Sometimes it was a lack of feeling safe with a paycheck and a job. Our children's education was sporadic at best. Our basic needs, as massive economic uncertainty gripped the planet, caused untold anxiety for the majority of the population. Our safety was perceived to be interrupted when much of the world dove into the elevated understanding and reaction to the lack of safety experienced by Black and BIPOC people suffering from systemic racism. Never before have we experienced so many things taking away our core sense of safety in such a short period of time. And never before has it been more important to scale conversations about people's sense of safety.

In the first month of the COVID-19 pandemic, Thought-Exchange usage doubled every 30 days; at times it was 1000 times higher than in the previous year. Safety was the predominant scaled conversation and it was led by thousands of people in all sectors.

Asking questions about safety seems scary but is actually extremely simple. As humans, most of us have developed an inherent ability to meet people where they are, one on one, with empathy. You don't have to be a trained psychologist or facilitator to understand the best sorts of question to ask people who are experiencing a lack of basic safety. Picture that person in front of you. You could be anywhere, a work event, a coffee shop, a family reunion. Here are the sorts of question you would likely instinctively ask them:

You must be going through a hard time, how are you?
What's on your mind?
What are your concerns?

Some variation on one of those questions would be at the tip of your tongue without thinking if you ran into someone you knew well who was managing the complexity of a global pandemic, worried about their job, concerned about their family, etc. If you are really in tune with that person, you'll instinctively validate their feelings instead of stepping over them. Despite this basic instinct, many leaders stumble in the moment while they consider how best to connect with a large group of hundreds or thousands who they know less well. That one-on-one instinct for validation can evaporate, and suddenly leaders consider skipping over asking what's on people's minds and instead ask them to focus on the positive, share silver linings and surface best practices. Doing this means forgetting how odd that would be in person, one-on-one. When safety is threatened, people need others to just ask what's on their mind. Full stop. Your basic instinct for the correct thing to do with that person in front of you, who is facing challenges, is what you need to trust when you scale up your conversations to include everyone.

Here are some questions you can ask large groups when they are going through safety challenges:

What's on your hearts and minds right now?
What are your thoughts and questions?
What are some fears or concerns you have about our situation?
What is most important to you given the news we just received?

These questions allow people to share their concerns and feel ok for having them. Validation doesn't mean problem-solving or justifying or rationalizing. Validating simply means helping people see that other reasonable people could have similar strong feelings in a similar situation. And that is helpful and builds connection. The basic fear is that people sharing concerns will not produce an outcome, but negativity is a fallacy. At the same time, it's important for leaders to realize there is work to be done, to be open to learning, and to empathize with people's concerns and fears at scale. I'll address that in a later chapter.

During the early days of the COVID pandemic we all got to understand a lot about people who felt a lack of safety and the impact of leaders willing to ask about concerns. Once safety is secured the next level is about structures.

STRUCTURE: HOW ARE THINGS GOING?

Structures are defined as the arrangements and relations between the elements of things. Think of them as the basic things you need to have and know in order to connect you with progress.

As the world transitioned into the hybrid model of office and remote work and learning during the first year of the COVID pandemic, almost all systems and structures were examined and change accelerated. Digital transformation during a pandemic is a great example of the second rung up the scaled conversations hierarchy of needs, because the example is so straightforward. Once our basic safety needs were met—initial questions about personal safety and job security—the next question was how to move forward and achieve basic progress. What does work look like? What does school look like? Is it online or face-to-face? Either way, how do we get there? What do we need when we arrive?

The same way the pandemic highlighted this progress from safety to structure, any event that causes a considerable change in structure puts a person, a group of people or entire organizations to the second rung of the ladder. Changing facilities, reorganizing teams, moving business online, reopening offices and on and on. In 2020, all of this had to happen within a matter of days or weeks.

What's important about the structure step is to ensure you, as a leader, ask about the structure in a way that attempts to empathize with the current state of things and to remove challenges so your team can experience self-worth. Fair warning: It's easy to accidentally turn structure conversations into vision conversations that alienate people if you are not careful.

Consider the difference between the two questions:

What are some successes, challenges and questions that are at the top of your mind as our facility moves to reopen?
And
What changes would best prepare our facilities for the future?

They are both about structures, but one is at the bottom of the hierarchy and the other is near the top. Can you see why? One is about checking in on the present moment and one assumes you are in a mindset to consider the future creatively. Imagine you experienced a small fire in your kitchen that caused you to have to renovate. During the renovations you are having a conversation with your partner/spouse/friend you share the house with. To see how they are doing amid the somewhat traumatic process, do you ask them: "How's it going with the new kitchen?" Or do you ask: "What other major renovations could we undertake to make our house even more awesome?"

Discussing big forward-looking change when structure is not established is triggering. It causes people to fight/flight/freeze. It retracts the safety established in the first step.

Instead, asking how people are feeling about the structural challenges they are facing in the near term and inviting them to consider challenges and opportunities other people are sharing can help them feel their needs will be met in a way that works for them. It can also help them empathize with other people struggling with similar challenges, which can be therapeutic.

Here are some questions you can ask groups going through structure challenges:

What thoughts do you have about our current work environment?
What are some challenges you are experiencing with our systems and processes?
What advice do you have for leadership right now?

By asking about people's current state without causing anxiety by dreaming too much about a future state, you can connect with people and help solve challenges to move everyone up the hierarchy. The challenge, of course, is being able to listen and take reasonable actions. But the good news is that if you achieve that you are able to move up to the next step: Connection.

CONNECTION: WHAT CAN WE DO TOGETHER?

Once the basic structures are addressed, or at least in motion, it's possible to begin to transition from "me" to think in terms of "we." This in itself is a major gift. Giving people the space and safety to express compassion for others allows them to experience compassion themselves. While this is extremely hard to do when they are in fight/flight/freeze mode, this can be an extremely powerful way to unite people and create shared purpose and experience when you have the chance.

Think of connection as a group of adventurers regrouping after a storm during an expedition. Safety has been established, shelters have been set up and now people are inside drinking tea (or maybe even margaritas). It's time to get a sense of what is important to "us" now. While the storm was raging and people were fighting for their safety and struggling to set up the shelter, it wasn't appropriate to ask: What should we do next? In the same way, when people are in the midst of enormous structural change you need to address those things *before* asking them to move up a level and talk about collective action.

Again, COVID-19 gave us a whirlwind class on this topic. Once structure was addressed after the first wave, and most of society was working from home, educating their kids from home and redesigning their lives at home, it became possible to think about how to do things together again. We planned small re-openings, distanced backyard BBQs, dinners with small groups, small group face-to-face meetings, vacations to close-by areas, online weddings, virtual family reunions, small group birthdays, etc. etc. This move from "me" to "we" is important to us as a highly social species. As we all learned during the pandemic, mental health crises and drug overdoses are highly correlated with isolation. The most dangerous place for a human to be is deeply alone.

As a leader it's important to identify those moments when changes have occurred, after basic needs have been met. Only then is it time to come together and discuss potential collective actions. Notice I said discuss potential actions and not decide the exact next step. As ever in conversation it is critical to think of questions in terms of broadening perspectives and surfacing insights, not in terms of democratizing decision-making.

At the same time, it is important to realize you are still quite low on the scaled conversations hierarchy. Consider the difference between these two questions:

What could we do together?
What advice do you have for things we can do better?

Can you see how the first one is emotionally grounding for some-one recently coming out of a crisis while the second one is not? The first question shows it's a collective effort toward collective action. The second puts the burden on the individual.

Picture that expedition team again, just inside the tent in the blus-tering storm, first sip of tea, first stress-free moment after a harrowing experience. The leader asks: What can we do to improve how we react better to a storm the next time? Too soon! You've established every-one is ok, the tent is up, so before working on aligning our team and improving, it's time to check in and connect.

Here are some questions leaders have asked to create connection:

What do we need to talk about today?
What is a story or example we need to hear today?
What do you want to share about your experience so far?

The key with the connection step is to stay in the place of hear-ing stories, sharing stories and experiences without the temptation to offer immediate solutions, and provide instant advice. Sticking in the stories, hopes and challenges for as long as possible while resisting the urge to drive ahead creates the fabric required to move up the hierarchy, at which time people will be motivated to solve their own challenges.

A critical aspect of the scaled conversations hierarchy is that it contains in it the core belief that people can be creative and drive transformation for themselves once they've found ways for basic needs to be met. That is different from the idea that you as a leader will be able to "transform them" if you can "move them" up the hierarchy by "meeting their needs." Remember that the hierarchy tool is not for engagement and is best understood as a tool to unify their inherent motivation and ability with the optimized direction of your organization by providing a platform for self-discovery. That begins to take focus at the alignment level.

ALIGNMENT: WHAT CAN WE IMPROVE?

Once your team or community is feeling connection, along with some level of personal safety and structure, you can look to optimize the next scaled conversations hierarchy: Alignment.

As a leader you can recognize the moment to initiate a conversation about alignment when you are setting new goals, adjusting budgets, considering new projects with new funding, etc. It is right in the middle of the hierarchy, and where many organizations spend most of their time in a typical year. Continuous improvement. Iteration. MVP culture. Lean methodology. Design thinking. All of these strategies and structures exist within the context that you have an organization and the organization's constituents need to be unified to optimize a future. This is a privileged place to be in an organization, so once everyone is at that level you need to leverage that privilege to drive change.

It is also important to recognize we are not at the top of the scaled conversations hierarchy yet. There are still problems. People have needs for tactics and survival strategies and efficiencies. Let's keep going with the analogy of our adventurers in the storm. At this point they have put the tea away and they are planning the route for the next leg of the journey. The storm caught everyone off guard and they don't want that to happen again. Maybe they have even packed up and are chatting together as they head down the next trail, trying to make sure the rest of the trip is successful despite the many unknowns.

To assess this layer of the hierarchy, consider the difference between these two questions:

What advice do you have for things we can improve?
And
What is possible now that wasn't possible before?

The first question asks for partnership in executing a task, and the second asks for partnership in dreaming. When there are new time pressures and changes causing challenges it's hard to shift yourself into a dreaming state. It feels like a waste of time. It causes anxiety because the "real work" isn't getting done and it feels like the vessel might crash into the rocks as its occupants gaze at the stars. The focus instead must remain on the here and now.

At the same time, everyone recognizes that good work is never done and after some amount of time spent addressing change and optimization people are yearning for a connection to a deeper purpose.

Here are some alignment questions leaders can ask to surface insights, earn tactical trust and ensure people are able to experience the best of one another and the best of their organizations:

> What can our organization do to best support our Black and/or BIPOC team members?
> What are some perspectives we might be missing?
> What advice do you have for things that we can improve?
> What do you need to be successful in the next six months?
> What do you want us to know about your work?
> How can we make our new initiative even more successful?
> One month has passed since we began, what reflections do you have on what is working well and what is not?
> What actions can we take to improve our communication?

The list for questions on this rung of the hierarchy is long and quite easy to develop. Are we doing something together as a team or community? Yes? Great. Then how can we do it better and make life easier for all of us?

The main issue in this level of the hierarchy is actually tone-setting and question design vs. emotional competency. The challenge here is to ensure questions are asked to gather voice, surface insights and avoid a false perception of democracy.

Consider the difference between these two questions:

> What is the single most important thing we need to do to support you right now?

And

What do you most need to be successful right now?

The first one sounds sharp and actionable—and it also strongly implies that you are voting on a single action and that action will be executed, likely at the expense of all of the other suggestions. So, participants will respond with the excitement of being handed control and with the expectation that the answer will be actioned. Answers like: "Give us more money!" are likely. Participants will think to themselves: You have one shot, why not take it?

In contrast, the second question doesn't suggest an abdication of control and is still open to ideas. Asking this question to a group of many people also implies we all need to consider the needs of one another because, of course, we can't do everything. The difference between voice and vote in the area of scaling conversations can't be emphasized enough.

By surfacing ideas, demonstrating listening, practicing clear communication about lessons learned and creating reasonable expectations around actions that will be taken, you are likely to experience successes. Those successes are achieved as a result of learning from the people who are also creating successes for themselves. This will earn you leadership capital. And the team or community you are leading is likely to be inspired to articulate what is working best between people, and what rules are causing success. It is then that you step up to the cultural level of the scaled conversations hierarchy.

CULTURE: WHAT ARE SOME OF THE BEST EXAMPLES OF US?

Getting to the place where you can work on improving your culture, for better or worse, requires you to have already experienced success. Culture is at the upper heights of the scaled conversations hierarchy. This is a helpful thing to realize if you have ever experienced frustration trying to "fix a toxic culture" by talking about the culture itself.

I feel culture is something that is often misunderstood. In organizations the idea of culture is often attached to words and ideals set forth by leaders during "strategic planning." But that doesn't really make sense. The culture of a country or region, or group of people, is something recognizable despite words and plans. It is the manifestation of the people in that environment. When you think of the best parts of the culture of an ethnic group, a region, or of a country you don't think of the rules set forth by leadership that are carefully abided by in order to create an optimal result. You think of all of the complex and delightful things you can see and describe. Culture isn't a pact or an agreement or a set of laws. It is nearly the opposite. It is the observation of all of the things that happen despite particular rules, laws or ambitions. The word culture, as it relates to the observable manifestations of a group of humans, conveys a similar meaning to the term culture when it is applied to culturing plants. It is about cultivating and growing, and focusing on particular aspects. As in organizations, when a culture is celebrated its key aspects thrive.

The culture of an organization is evident when it is either extremely broken, and people feel like leaving, or when it is exceptionally strong and people apply maximum discretionary effort. In either case, the word describes the experiences and aspects of an organization which are not related to any particular strategy or mission.

To discuss an organization's culture is really to amplify what is working best and recognize what we don't want to do. This is quite distinct from setting a vision, or practicing continual improvement, which are the very peak of the scaled conversations hierarchy.

Consider the difference between these three questions:

What do we say and do to one another in our organization when we are at our very best?
And
What do we need to do together to be successful next year?
And
Imagine its five years from now and we are the most successful we have ever been as an organization. What is working and why?

The first question is about drawing focus to things that already exist. It is a question about culture. The second is about improving things that don't work. It is about alignment. The final question is about designing the future. It is about vision.

The important thing to understand about culture is the significance of recognizing those moments that need to be celebrated, articulated, and therefore perpetuated. This creates shared culture, and shared culture can move mountains. When people feel part of a strong culture it is because they see a lot of success and have the stories and language to articulate it. Milan, Italy, has a strong coffee culture. The shops are busy with passionate people and I have experienced the coffee to be excellent and the conversations to be lively. The Apple store has a strong customer culture. After closing time, no less than two different employees, on two different occasions, opened the door for me, helped me solve a problem, and took time to connect with me personally, even though the store had officially closed 15 minutes ago.

The magic of culture is not magic at all. It is about cultivation. When members of an organization report a "toxic culture" it is important to back up a few levels in the hierarchy and realize people are not ready to talk about culture! If they are experiencing a toxic culture, they are also likely to be encountering safety or structural challenges that need to be addressed. By going back in the hierarchy and working through the steps to where you can achieve alignment, and therefore success, you earn the right to work on improving your culture by nurturing it and highlighting it.

Here are some questions leaders have asked to cultivate culture:

What are some short stories or examples of moments that best describe our culture?
What is most important to you about our culture?
What are the sorts of things we do and say when we are at our very worst?—and then? What are the things we can say and do to one another to help us be at our very best?

What are some big mistakes we have made together that need to be celebrated to help us remember it's important to make mistakes and learn?

What is a story we most need to hear about a success we have created together?

What is an action or a solution someone has implemented that needs to be celebrated?

These sorts of questions require a high level of trust, a history of at least some shared success and a unified sense of purpose. Organizations do well to maintain culture through consistent questions on successes and failures when things are working. The trigger for cultural conversations is when you are moved or impacted by the achievements of your team or community.

The time to NOT have a conversation about culture is when you feel in your heart it is broken or non-existent. Leaders have a temptation to want to ask about cultural success when instead they need to meet people where they are at.

Imagine you are a disheartened person inside an underperforming organization, with a culture you would describe as "toxic." Now, take a deep breath and consider the difference between these two questions:

What are the aspects of our cultural tenets of respect, grit and imagination we most need to apply to our work right now?
And
What's on your heart and mind right now?

Even in this fictitious situation you can instantly feel the difference between a leader willing to meet you where you are (the second question: Safety) as opposed to one who seeks to "remind you of the amazing culture" that is likely written on a plaque somewhere, gathering dust (the first question).

Another scenario to consider is when, in your heart, you felt the culture was strong but, on asking a culture question, you discovered that people were not where you thought they were. What happens then? The risk is simply that you won't have the conversation you were hoping for. Imagine you are struggling because you heard a rumor you might lose your job. Or, imagine you heard a rumor affecting your physical safety and you now don't feel comfortable in your work environment. In that state of mind, if a leader asks you "What is most important about our culture?," your answer is probably some version of "I prefer cultures where people tell me if I have a job tomorrow." Or, "I don't feel safe—are we going to address <insert rumor>?" You'll get a conversation in any event and, if you understand and practice the scaled conversations hierarchy, you'll know what to do next. Leaders earn trust when they err on the side of being willing to lead a conversation when things are unknown vs. when they are shut down, afraid to ask questions due to fear of the answers.

If you have done the work, you have aligned your team or community and you are seeing success, there is no greater gift to your organization than to celebrate the accomplishments of your culture. It's the reason for being. It's fireworks on a warm summer night in the town square. It's the winter carnival parade. It's a peaceful protest that resulted in positive change. It's a slideshow montage about your last vacation set to music. Conversations about culture are celebrations about what makes us "Us." And we need to have a lot of them whenever we create the environment for them to succeed.

Once people experience collective recognition and opportunity to articulate shared stories and language they are elevated to a place where they can envision an even better world tomorrow. Defining culture prepares the soil for vision.

VISION: IMAGINE THE FUTURE

After people feel a sense of accomplishment it becomes possible to dream about self and organizational actualization. Vision is defined as the state of being able to see. This state is a privilege and its one that many organizations fight very hard to earn.

Consider someone who has just arrived at the door of an offsite retreat where a team is gathering inside about to discuss the mission and vision of the organization. If you lead a large team or community, you have likely attended or hosted one of these events. Let's unpack this person standing at the door, ready to dream, from a hierarchy perspective. Consider all of the rungs of the hierarchy that were addressed to get that person here.

There's an assumption that the organization is safe and structures are in place. The simple fact this person is present shows they are valued; they have created enough alignment that successes occurred resulting in acknowledgement. The fact that this is an "offsite" event prevents them from accidentally sliding back down the hierarchy levels as they encounter daily challenges pulling them back to the first levels of safety and structures. Now, at this retreat, the food is good, the recreation time is planned and controlled, the advice of the organizer is invariably: "Turn off your distractions and ensure everyone knows you are unavailable. You normally work in the organization; this is a special time to work on the organization."

All of the planning, framing, food, activities, fresh air, nice views, etc., associated with this retreat are designed for one reason: To manufacture the optimal environment that gives people permission to think about the future with imagination. To see with wisdom.

In the same way, your work leading conversations that allow your team and/or community to rise up the scaled conversations hierarchy can be considered a conscious effort to create the environment to imagine a future together.

While it is nice to attend those face-to-face events, they are analog events with emotional underpinnings that can be successfully replicated online where hundreds and even thousands of people instead gather in a virtual space. When you want to discuss vision, it is important to recognize that the setting has to be optimized for collaborative dreaming, and as many challenges and successes as possible need to be addressed to create the ideal environment.

Scaling conversations at each level of the hierarchy creates this possibility with entire teams and organizations. At the beginning of this book, I discussed leadership capital. Visionary conversations happen best when the relationship, process and ownership banks are full. People feel related, they understand and participate in decision-making processes, and they feel unity and ownership over the direction of the organization. Rather than wonder which one of these things is most important to create a successful organization, it's critical to realize that the real success comes from generating all three at the same time.

Once your relationship, process and ownership capital banks are full, and you are firing on all three cylinders as it were, you are ready to discuss vision. Here are some questions leaders ask to dive into vision:

Imagine it's <insert number of months or years> in the future and things are very successful. What is happening and why is it working so well?

What are we building together and why is it important?

What are the most important qualities and attributes of an ideal graduate 10 years from now?

Where could we be five years from now if we did everything right?

What successes from today do we need to focus on as we dream about the future?

How will we know we are successful as an organization five years from now?

Large-scale conversations about vision are critical if you want to create large-scale success. They are also dangerously dreamy. If people feel the leader's privilege to ask questions about the future is unearned, they will disengage. Countless strategic planning processes fail to create meaningful participation when a privileged group of leaders reaches out to "engage" those who could be in any state of insecurity. You've probably received surveys yourself, asking you to drop what you are doing and dream as a part of the next ten-year strategic plan of some organization you are loosely affiliated with. Statistically speaking, you probably didn't participate. You probably had a chance to attend a meeting or a town hall you didn't go to and you were probably sent a survey you didn't open. Not many people participate in these things. And the reason is wrapped in the scaled conversations hierarchy. In the past, few leaders had the skills and tools to build leadership capital at scale and create an environment in which people can think about the future together. Luckily, that is changing, as more and more leaders prioritize the voices of their teams and communities.

One distinction to help clarify the rung of the vision hierarchy level is best revealed by considering the difference between these two questions:

What does success look like for us five years from now?
And
What are some things we could do to disrupt ourselves and completely change our model to succeed exponentially?

The first question is about gathering voices and dreaming about a common future. It is about vision. The second is about maximum creativity and is about transformation (the next and top level of the hierarchy). The difference between these two can be subtle, but like any layer of the hierarchy it is dangerous to mistake one for the other.

Imagine that person standing at the door of the retreat center feeling that the current vision of their organization, or the organization itself, is out of date; that person is excited that he or she has been invited to help set the organization's direction for the next five years. However, after walking in the door they find the room is filled with strange drawings and people talking about completely unfamiliar topics: How can we change everything? How can we disrupt ourselves? What can we blow up and reimagine? This person is likely to be propelled back down to the bottom of their ladder of needs, thinking some variant of: What's wrong? Why are we changing everything? Where are we headed?

The issue is that, without a clear vision of the future, imagining everything to be different is likely to trigger a reaction. Imagine you own a house with someone and that person finds you on your computer looking at real estate listings in a faraway town you have never discussed. This is either a scary or fun thing for your partner. Scary if they feel you suddenly want to move to an unknown place for unknown reasons. Fun if they feel you have a shared vision for where you might be for the next few years and you're simply dreaming alternate realities or imagining a different future. What state do you and your partner need to be in to casually imagine flipping your life upside down? You need to have established a shared vision. And every other rung in the hierarchy. Radical transformation is not shared vision. But it's potentially very exciting once the right to dream has been earned and a shared future is real.

TRANSFORMATION: WHAT IS POSSIBLE?

Transformation is defined as a radical, thorough, dramatic change. Think caterpillar to butterfly. Cars instead of horses. Internet instead of the telegraph. Transformation is about under-taking or -going extreme reimagining. It is the very tippity tip of the scaled conversations hierarchy. It is the realm of a human who prepares for death and embraces birth. Organizations that undergo things they label transformations are usually changing something big. Digital transformation is a common phrase, and either an aspiration or critical success factor for most businesses. It's about completely reimagining things with maximum creativity. Einstein famously said that, given a set amount of time to solve a problem, he'd spend most of it getting clear on the question. In the same way, transformation is really dependent on creating a shared understanding of why it needs to occur in the first place.

Humor me: Set this book down and with your right hand make the shape of a gun, like this:

Notice it has one barrel, a trigger at the top. Now, with your left hand, make bunny ears, like this:

Notice the bunny only has two ears and the rest is wrapped in. The gun in your right hand represents an Elmer Fudd-like character and the ears in your left hand represent a Bugs Bunny-like bunny. The thing about Elmer and Bugs is they tend to chase each other around and, at some point, Elmer ends up with rabbit ears on, and Bugs ends up holding the gun.

To symbolize this, switch hands so the gun is your left and the ears are your right like this:

Got it? Now switch them back again.

Notice the bunny is supposed to only have two ears....Not three. And the gun doesn't have a weird kickstand or a second barrel. Two ears, one barrel. Keep trying:

And then:

Try to do it relatively quickly. Keep trying this at least 20 times.

Now let's unpack that exercise.

People fall roughly into three categories.

Category 1 = **Nope.**

   I asked you to put down the book and make bunny ears and you thought to yourself: Nope. Won't do that. My hands are preoccupied. And I am busy reading, thank you very much. So, you just kept reading.

Category 2 = One and done.

   I asked you to put down the book and try to switch bunny ears and a gun and you tried it once. Then you kept reading, telling yourself, I probably get the point of the exercise but

I don't need to do it again. Intellectually I can understand that seemed hard or something and I am ready for whatever is coming next. Let's get on with it.

Category 3 = Mastery Machines.

This group of people, the smallest of the three categories by far, has a deep and largely irrational need to master any new thing. If you are in this category, you went back and forth over and over until new neural pathways were built and switching back and forth between Bugs and Elmer is effortless. This group will probably send me a DM in Twitter or LinkedIn to proclaim their newfound expertise. It took this group of people far more than 20 tries to switch back and forth from bunny to gun and they were surprised just how hard it was, just how many times the gun had a kickstand, etc., before the new ability locked into place. But then it locked in.

This is probably the very simplest transformation you can experience. All of us know how to make a gun, all of us know how to make bunny ears, but this is likely the first time you have attempted to go back and forth between the two so you are actually creating the neural pathways in your body to send signals to your hands to do that. The effort of learning that silly skill is a great example of transformation broken down to a very basic level. The transformation is the new bond between your brain and your hands that, like riding a bike, will likely be established for life after you master this little skill. A new thing that a moment ago wasn't there.

Here is what is really important about transformation: We all have people on our teams or in our communities who fit into one of the three categories: Nope, One and Done and Mastery Machines. Any radical change you ask to transform will be met with resistance and skepticism by most and acceptance by a very small group of early adopting types of people who jump onto every new thing.

That brings me to the golden ratio of change: **1:10**

The 1 is the **what** of a change and the 10 is the **why**.

This image needs to be glued to the back of the eyelids of every leader and it's something I still mess up all the time. Any change you are thinking of driving needs to be described as "why" an entire order of magnitude more than "what" if you hope to get people on board. Otherwise, they will be like the majority of you, who chose to not put the book down to learn something new to do with your fingers. If I had bothered to describe ten well-thought-out and relatively strong reasons why this Bugs and Elmer exercise was critical to your personal development and our shared success, I would have had a chance of getting most of you on board from the start (assuming we were together on the same level of the hierarchy where we can experiment with new ideas). Most changes that create challenges have a lot of uncertainty around the "Why?"

The reason I discuss Bugs Bunny when discussing success at scaling conversations about transformation is to point out that humans are a paradox. We are wired to not radically change things and to be fearful of rapid transformation. Establish safety, protect the core. We are also wired to evolve and we seek transformative experiences in our relationships with our partners, religions and organizations.

Creating competency at driving innovation and transformation is about recognizing the need to work all the way up to the top of the hierarchy to a place where you have shared vision. From there you ask Why? Why would we want to transform? Why do we need change? Why now? Why us? Why not? By asking ourselves these questions and gleaning answers we have the ingredients for scaling conversations about transformation.

At the top of the scaled conversations hierarchy nothing is easy but everything is possible. Imagine the people who invented democracy, the internet, the airplane, etc., etc., etc. Imagine the privilege and the urgency required to drive change. All innovations are met with fear and awe and then one day you'll be sitting on an airplane, about to vote on your handheld device along with 90% of the population in a secure online election while the airplane is lifting off and you don't even look out the window or crack a smile. It's just normal. Remember when we didn't have smartphones? Remember when democracy was analog and we had to mail in ballots or vote in person? Imagine our grandparents who didn't have the internet and didn't fly around the world? Hard to picture. And if you are wondering, yes, I put electronic voting there so you can experience the fear and/or excitement of a yet-embraced transformation likely to occur in our near future. That feeling of imagining a world that votes almost entirely online inspires a mixture of complex emotions. Such is the nature of transformation.

Asking questions about transformation is about embracing the unknown and taking joy in thinking radically.

Here are some questions to ask about transformation:

What is possible for us now that wasn't possible until recently? And why?

What would we do if we had unlimited resources? And why?

What are some new things we could do together that are completely unlike anything we've done before? And why could we do them?

What are some problems we don't solve currently but maybe should?

These are all questions about the unknown and they are challenging to have at scale because incremental improvement sneaks in.

To lock in the distinction of transformation consider the difference between these two questions:

What is maybe possible now that wasn't possible before?
And
What new things could we do to improve the work we do together?

The first question is about transformation and the second about alignment. But if people are not in the space of understanding the "Why?" of transformation and how it relates to shared vision, the answers to both questions will be about incremental improvement. In fact, many, if not most, attempts to scale conversations about transformation result in conversations about continuous improvement. It is easier, more comfortable and more applicable to focus there. Only by getting clear about the rationale for transformation and sharing the why in ten different ways as you build on your vision can you dream to achieve transformative conversations at scale.

That said, unifying your team and community in a conversation about transformation is a challenging and rare opportunity and it is the place where new possibilities emerge, new service models are dreamed up, new partnerships initiated—and even where entirely new organizations are born. Earning your ability to lead that conversation is a powerful professional aspiration.

As with any model, applying the lessons learned through dissecting the scaled conversations hierarchy will be much less linear than a neat ladder you simply climb. It's important to realize that one group of people is not necessarily in any particular level of the hierarchy as a whole. Different topics, subjects, initiatives all have their own hierarchy associated with them. As I read Bob Iger's book, *The Ride of a Lifetime*, I tried to imagine a hint of what it would be like launching an entire Disney park in Asia (Vision) on the same day he was dealing with a mass shooting in Orlando (Safety). You never know what someone is going through. A single person can be on more than one level at one time. In 2020 I tried my best as CEO of ThoughtExchange to lead enormous usage growth (Alignment) during the pandemic (Safety) while nursing broken ribs and collar bone (Safety) and at the same time taking a stand to ensure we conspire with people to help us become a successful anti-racist organization (All levels from Safety to Transformation) while we raised capital to prepare for a likely recession (Structure). Many times, these initiatives overlapped and on any one day we might be celebrating, grieving, dreaming and planning depending on the issue.

Mastering leading conversations is about mastering your ability to meet people where they are at on any given topic on any given day. Achieving good judgement can only really be gained through experience. And experience, again, often comes from bad judgement. By using the scaled conversations hierarchy, you have the tools to try to get it right with your team or community. As a leader it is really important to not be afraid of getting it wrong. Doing something is better than doing nothing.

This was a very detailed—necessarily detailed—discussion of the scaled conversations hierarchy. I provided some sample questions that can be asked within each level of the hierarchy. But what actually makes a question good for a scaled conversation? I delve into that next.

CHAPTER 9

Components of Good Questions for Scaled Conversations

N ow that we've covered why, and to some degree when, to ask questions through the lens of meeting people where they are at, let's touch on how. Each section of the scaled conversations hierarchy in the previous chapter has some questions that serve as good examples of simple ways to tackle complex subjects.

The "How?" of constructing a good question for a scaled conversation is actually the easiest part once you realize how to meet people where they are at. The question itself is not as important as the intention, timing and communication around the initiative. That said, there are a few tenets to consider as you lean in to understand how to ask great questions. The components I'll cover are:

1. Openness

2. Candor

3. Consider and rate thoughts of others

4. Avoid a false democracy

5. Meet people where they are at!

Let's start with openness.

OPENNESS

Consider that the state of being open is the state of allowing access. When it comes to developing questions the important thing to consider is that any question you ask needs to allow access for voice. Pragmatically, asking an open-ended question means avoiding binary choices like: Which one do you like best?

What is more important is considering what you are open to. It is easy to really mess up a question by adding what you believe are helpful pieces of context. All this does is make people feel less invited to share their minds. Consider the difference between these two questions:

> We've been working remotely now for six months. What are some challenges and successes you've had with your physical work environment, your communication with your colleagues and your daily tasks?
> And
> What challenges and successes have you experienced since we began working remotely?

They are both open questions. But the second question allows people to say anything without pre-supposing the topic areas that are most important. It also sounds like something one person would ask another person. A good guide to asking open questions at scale is to imagine asking a single human that question face-to-face. Forcing people to respond within specific categories is a very unnatural way of speaking yet many leaders consider asking things of many people they would never ask of a single person.

Openness is being open to what people need to say. The best open questions are simple.

> What challenges have you experienced?
> What advice do you have?
> What are examples of us at our best?
> What hopes do you have?

The best way to access openness is to consider what I discuss in the next section: Candor.

CANDOR

This is the quality of being open in expression. Candor is what is required to ask excellent open-ended questions.

I once spoke with a small group of executives at a large firm with many engineers. We were discussing questions to ask their employees. As a group, they asked me how to ask questions about people's sense of alignment with the vision of the organization, their level of job satisfaction, etc. Their first idea was to ask everyone approximately ten questions, ranging from things like overall happiness to sense of accomplishment to challenges with their work environment. I was not getting an overall sense of candor from them so I started asking: "Why?"

It sounded something like this:

We want to ask our staff ten questions.
Why?
Because we want to find out what they think is important about their happiness and work environment.
Why?
Because we want to uncover any issues they are feeling right now.
Why?
Because we don't want good people to leave our organization.
Why?
Because a large group of them just did. All at once.
Ah. Why?
Well, that's just it... we don't know.
... Why?
Well, because I guess we haven't asked them.

Bingo.

Now, understanding the root of what they wanted, I suggested they frame a question by saying something like this: "As you know we just had a large group of employees leave and we'd like advice to ensure that doesn't happen again." I then suggested the question was something like: What advice do you have to help us ensure we can retain our staff?

That was the open and candid question. Just ask it. One of the executives asked me: "Can we really just ask that?" To which I responded: "Yes. And isn't that the question you would like to be asked if it was your colleagues who left?" Yes, it was. It's honest and acknowledges there are things, obviously, the organization needed to learn. That acknowledgment is actually the hardest part.

I am a big fan of the "Five Whys" analysis technique, which is what I used in the above example. In a nutshell, this is where you keep asking "Why?" until you get to a root issue beneath a more obvious symptom. Applying the Five Whys concept, or Three Whys, or however many Whys you need to get to the root cause, is the foundation of creating questions that elicit candor.

Usually, a trigger for wanting to ask a group a question is a challenge you are experiencing or expecting to experience in the future. And candidly talking about that challenge has the ability to generate all kinds of actionable insights while generating leadership capital. One of the best ways for someone to feel respected is when a leader they trust or admire asks for their advice. Consider that, as you are wondering just how "candid" to be with your challenges.

Another bit of useful framing I heard was from the leader of a large public organization. He wanted to ask everyone about a contentious topic related to funding a project worth hundreds of millions of dollars which would affect everyone in a big way. His senior leadership team was skeptical about leading a conversation on such a polarizing and impactful topic. Someone asked him: "Should we really start this conversation?" To which he replied: "We're not starting it. It is already happening." People are always talking about everything, especially things like this. When we ask the question, we just get to be part of the conversation.

The same concept applies to the conversation with the executives at the company with the engineers who had left. The truth is that everyone in the organization was already talking about the large group of employees who had left. By asking a candid question about why, and how to prevent it happening again, the leadership was able to be part of that conversation.

Candor is one of the most underrated leadership skills. Many may confuse it with bluntness and fearlessness, but candor is neither. It is the quality of being open in expression, which often means sharing fears, concerns and vulnerabilities rather than sharp feedback. Without candor, the next component of a question—considering the thoughts of others—won't happen.

CONSIDER THE THOUGHTS OF OTHERS

This component is tricky. To ask a single question at scale it has to be both personally meaningful and apply to a larger group. To ask a question to a large group requires you to think in terms of "We."

To dive into this, consider the difference between these two questions:

What are three key challenges we need to address?
And
What are some key challenges we need to address?

They seem very similar—just a single word of difference—but in the context of a conversation, the first question asks people to share three ideas. The next step would then be for other people to consider and rate the three responses as a group. It becomes bizarre really quickly because people don't agree in groups of thoughts. Imagine asking about ice cream:

What are the three best flavors of ice cream?

- Chocolate, vanilla, cookies and cream

- Chocolate, cookies and cream and rocky road.

- Cookies and cream, vanilla and espresso gelato.

It becomes more like a matching exercise and it is really impossible to agree with a group of things. This is a really subtle thing that becomes critical at scale. Questions have to result in singular answers that can be evaluated one at a time.

Asking questions to allow for considering the thoughts of others, they also need to contain the notion of group agreement. Consider the difference between these two questions:

What is a solution you have used and have found very effective?
And
What are some potentially effective solutions to this challenge?

They are both good questions, but once you imagine everyone considering and rating the thoughts of other people, you can see that only the second one makes sense to rate at scale. The first asks for your personal past experience of a specific solution. Then, when you rate you will see new solutions from other people and you will be asked: What is a solution you have used and have found very effective? Of course, not everyone has tried every single solution so people will be forced to "pass" or "skip" almost all thoughts. In the second question you will see a solution you have never thought of before and then you'll be asked to agree with each solution with this question: What are some potentially effective solutions to this challenge? You can rate 100% of the thoughts based on how much you agree with the potential. This is a subtle but important concept.

Though there are infinite variations on this theme, the core principle is this:

When you ask a question, don't put yourself in the context of a singular person answering the question. Instead, put yourself in the shoes of someone reading and assessing the thoughts of other people. Does your question make sense from that context? What needs to change to make it work?

Conversations are the realm of surfacing insight, discovering common ground, ensuring people feel heard, etc. They are not in the realm of group deciding and voting. That is not the purpose of scaled conversations and what I will discuss next.

AVOID A SENSE OF FALSE DEMOCRACY

This one is big.

There are two excellent examples of the challenge of group democracy that hit the media in recent years. The first was Boaty McBoatface. This was a UK crowdsourced process where people answered a question about naming an expensive research vessel for the Natural Environment Research Council. Boaty McBoatface won by a landslide. It was funny. But the less funny part was summed up by the headline in the Guardian by the NERC Chief:

NERC chief has final say and faces dilemma between credibility of the organization and burden of public opinion

Ouch. Credibility and public opinion put on opposite sides of a fence…when the truth is harnessing accurate public opinion isn't a burden. It is only a burden when you do it wrong. If this was an interest-based question about potential names and why they were potentially a fit, this would have been a huge success. The locus of decision-making control was always with the NERC Chief but the question implied, by its nature, that it wasn't. In the end there is now a little onboard submarine named Boaty McBoatface aboard the more grandly named vessel: The Sir David Attenborough.

In a similar and maybe even more entertaining example, Walmart held a competition to see which Walmart store had the most fans as measured by the most Facebook likes in a certain period of time. The winning store received a free, local, Pitbull concert. When Pitbull found himself in the most remote Walmart location on earth, Kodiak, Alaska, thanks to the collective sense of humor of the internet, he did a great job of following through on his commitment and showing that the public voice wasn't a burden at all. Getting to Kodiak might have been. But the residents of Kodiak appreciated both the support of the internet and the effort put into the concert in the end.

Both of these situations had the same dynamic. Large organizations created a moment where they democratized a decision and people therefore took advantage of it.

Scaling conversations is not about the most common answer winning. Consider the difference between these two questions:

What should we do about our problem?
And
What are your thoughts about how we can solve our problem?

The first question implies the group might be given the right to do whatever they decide together; the second question invites everyone to contribute their thinking in a more curious way.

Consider the difference between these two words:

Can (be able)
And
Should (indicates obligation)

Asking "can" in a question implies You, or the collective We, will "be able." By contrast, "should" indicates obligation. In many questions, simply replacing the word "should" with "can" changes the context of the question and keeps the locus of decision making clearly out of the realm of voting.

Overall, the same insight of considering and dissecting the small-group, analog version of a situation helps you scale effectively.

A leader asking a small group of trusted advisors for advice on how to solve a challenge uses language like:

What are your thoughts on these scenarios?
What can we potentially do?
What am I not thinking of?
What do you think people want?
What has your experience been?

Very rarely does a leader ask a question to a group of advisors that sounds like this:

What should I do exactly?
What action must I take?
Which solution do I need to pick?
What three things do I need to do first?

Leaders who ask those kinds of questions to people affected by their decisions are clearly not in control. They are looking to rid themselves of a decision instead of facilitating a discussion that will help them lead the process of defining actions and solutions. On the other side of questions such as these are things like blame and detachment. "If the group voted for a terrible idea, well, it wasn't my fault." Or: "I went with the majority so, if it blows up, don't ask me for help."

A final point of clarification: There is a rather critical place for democracy in our society and that is in our system of government. Saying it is not appropriate to "falsely democratize decision-making" doesn't mean further establishing democracy, and protecting it in our society, isn't important; nor that the global fight for it isn't the most pressing issue facing our species. Democracy is simply defined as a system of government by all members. Most organizations are not that. Collaborative negotiation and interest-based discussions are the most important things leaders can do to earn leadership capital and leverage the power of the voice of their people.

Finally, we come to the last component of a question, and where so many of the underpinnings of scaled conversations lie: meeting people where they are at.

MEETS PEOPLE WHERE THEY ARE AT

Questions need to meet people where they are at. This is the final section of this chapter because it is worth repeating. Steps 1 through 4 of how to ask great questions are all nuance and detail of the higher-level concept that organizations have needs that must be met. Asking questions to genuinely understand how to meet those needs will guide you in the right direction. Thinking very hard about the needs of people in terms of the scaled conversations hierarchy helps you be open and candid at scale while avoiding false democracy. No one wants to be perceived as closed, deceitful, small and out of control. Thinking hard about the language you use can reveal a lot of what you really want compared to what you appear to want.

As an example of this, consider these two questions:

What should we do?
And
What should we do?

Same question, same mistake of "should" in both, and let's consider them asked to the same group of people at different times.

Imagine you are in an organization that just had its offices shut down in the early days of the COVID-19 pandemic. The day after the shutdown everyone was supposed to be heading to an offsite location for a large meeting of 100 or so people. Time is of the essence. 100 people are traveling tomorrow morning. A rapidly changing situation. As a part of that, the leader sends out an emergency question to all 100 people and shares that obviously this is a very complex time, they want to hear the opinion of absolutely everyone within the next 30 minutes, and asks, in a hurry: What should we do?

Now imagine that this same leader is launching a new initiative with the sales team. A new product with new pricing is being released and it has many complex factors to get right. Ahead of the launch the leader explains this is an exciting new product, and even a new era for the organization. They want to engage everyone prior to rolling out this initiative. The leader asks: What should we do?

In the first scenario everyone was panicked, including the leader, and rightfully so. Asking the wrong question and including "should" instead of "can," implying group decision making, not nailing the hierarchy, etc., is.... Forgivable. No problem. A leader met their team where they were at. It was an honest attempt with forgivable flaws.

In the second scenario there is no emergency. But by asking "What should we do?" the leader has launched an entire buffet of problems. Does the leader mean they don't know what they are doing? Is this fake engagement just to look good? How could it be that no one knows what we are doing? Are we turning our strategy into a vote? That's scary. The leader didn't meet people where they were at and instead confused everyone. A simple change of language would have been successful though: What are your thoughts and questions about our new product? Or: "What advice do you have as we roll out this new product?" Depending where people are at on the scaled conversations hierarchy, there are many different questions that will work.

The difference between the same question in the two scenarios is authenticity. Honest mistakes are easy to forgive, and someone acting less than optimally in a time of stress is better than them doing nothing at all. Accidentally democratizing a question when the situation is obviously tactical and not moving fast can have far worse results. And if you dig into it, the only reason someone would ask "What should we do?" in the second situation is probably because they are actually being disingenuous or are completely disorganized.

CHAPTER 10

Synthesizing Scaled Conversations

S caling conversations that successfully surface insight from many people has one major, final, component. You need to be willing to listen. And learn. And take appropriate action whenever necessary. This is easier said than done. It is easier to say that the firehose of feedback you received was so vast it is impossible to trust and turn into action. When you surface actual insight in the form of candid thoughts prioritized by many people, you need to dig in and unlock the value. This isn't a burden. Far from it. It's a skillset you selfishly need to acquire to make sure you can experience all of the tangible and intangible value of inclusion at scale.

Learning how to scale conversations is a process. Learning how to identify the hierarchy of scaled conversations and move between them takes time. So, it only makes sense that understanding how to approach evaluating what comes out of a scaled conversation also requires a skill set. There's a five-step process to synthesizing what occurs in a scaled conversation, and those steps are what I'll walk you through in this chapter.

1. Create a representational dissemination group

2. Overcome reptilian survival brain

3. Demonstrate listening and learning

4. Adopt language

5. Commit to action (even if the action is to take none)

CREATE A REPRESENTATIONAL DISSEMINATION GROUP

Representation is interesting. Representation itself is defined as the act of acting or speaking on behalf of someone. Most initiatives that involve making big decisions that affect many people involve the formation of a representation committee. For example, a small group of diverse people are consulted in DE+I initiatives and meant to represent all people of color. Or a small group of salespeople is consulted to represent the whole sales team when big changes are happening. Or a small group of community members is gathered to represent the larger community when cities and school districts need to make decisions impacting taxpayers. Normally some effort is made to ensure the demographics of the small group represents the larger group.

In these scenarios the people gathered are meant to "be" the voice of the larger community through representation. Different ideas and scenarios are presented to this group for their feedback and advice. Overall, it is better to have this kind of group than nothing at all but it is extremely challenging to actually find people who can appropriately and accurately represent others. If I'm being honest, it's actually impossible. People are so unique, and have so many different components to what makes them an individual, that representing them with someone who looks similar to them, or has a similar position to them, doesn't work and doesn't build trust.

This mechanism of a representative committee only makes sense when you can't actually reach out and hear the unbiased voices of the larger group. When you can effectively scale conversations, it is important to start your synthesizing journey by expanding the group of people who can help you listen, learn and disseminate the results.

By shifting the idea of a representative group to a representational dissemination group you are sending two strong messages:

1. All voices are important in the conversation so the key opportunities for input are not confined to a small group but open to everyone.

2. Authentically listening and sharing insights from the results of the scaled conversation is complex and requires different perspectives to ensure everyone's voice is considered and actioned as effectively as possible.

A representational dissemination group can do an excellent job of helping leadership consider the top thoughts in the scaled conversation and then provide advice on ways to apply and share knowledge. This increases insight, as well as trust. And it reduces potential conflict and unnecessary politics as people realize the group selected to helped disseminate results to the people who need the outcomes.

This can be done either formally or informally but the key is to reach out to a group of people and ask for help understanding the larger group. And remember to share publicly that you are open to doing so.

After you have results and a group of people to help you understand them, you need a reminder that learning new things will likely trigger you and tempt you to into fight, flight or freeze mode.

OVERCOME REPTILIAN SURVIVAL BRAIN

The human brain is a wonder. What we know about it pales in comparison to what scientists still don't know. What has had a lot of research is how the brain kicks in its survival mechanism. When we detect a threat, our brain has a structure that controls a lot of our self-preservation behavior patterns. When we encounter unfamiliar things, our brain is first to respond and gets a sort of priority over our other brain functions as a means of self-defense. This takes the form of fight, flight or freeze. You can imagine this has significant positive benefits out in the wild if we encounter something that could be a lion and that thing that could be a lion may seek to harm us. Best to not engage a lion-like thing in empathetic dialogue as a first response when we may simply be eaten in the next moment. In life-or-death situations for animals, mere seconds can be critical and the brain therefore has the ability to ensure a decisive reaction at a time of threat.

What serves us animals well for survival, however, is a challenge when it comes to uncovering new perspectives and actively overcoming conscious and unconscious bias. Inclusive leaders who practice scaling conversations encounter new and unexpected things all. the. time. After all, what's the point of including diverse voices if we don't elevate the unexpected and expose ourselves to typically unheard voices?

It would be great to report that open and inclusive leaders have an equally open and inclusive mind that instantly overcomes their survival brain when they encounter unexpected or unanticipated perspectives. But that's simply not true. The survival brain is built in. Hardwired. When we encounter new information that challenges our world view, in the slightest, it is triggered. Even the first instinct of the most experienced leader scaling conversations may be to say "Oh no, that'll never work!" when confronted with new ideas and free-flowing thoughts. I'll give you a few examples.

A leader asks everyone what they want to discuss at an upcoming leadership meeting. The leader is expecting strategies and tactics. The responses that are elevated make it clear that, on the whole, people are feeling quite demotivated; they express frustration that they were not included in recent decisions that affect them. And these decisions are slowing down revenue. What do you think the leader feels? Do they feel thankful to have uncovered something they hadn't expected? Excited to unlock revenue by understanding what was missed when changes were rolled out? Curious?

Nope.

Chances are they feel... Ticked off. Mad. Upset. Frustrated. Don't these people understand they are lucky to have a job? Don't they know how fortunate they are to have a leader who cares what they think in the first place? In other organizations they wouldn't even have a voice!!?! And so on and so forth.

This is thanks to our survival brain. As soon as we feel threatened as leaders, a weird self-preservation thing occurs. The truer the response from people, the sharper the sting. The sharper the sting, the worse the survival response kicks in. Consider what a pain in the butt that is! The more you learn, the less you are able to learn it!

The most important thing to do with your survival brain is to acknowledge it. Once you do that, you can see and feel yourself reacting in a predictable way. Even if that way is less than optimal, noticing yourself behave that way gives you a golden thing: Choice. With the ability to choose your actions you can choose to . . . take a deep breath. Hear your internal voice rant a bit. Wait for the survival instinct to recede and for compassion and logic to swell in.

I am not a great example of an altruistic leader who has the quick ability to compassionately transform new ideas into change. I have acquired some muscle though. As someone who regularly uses an inclusion tool to bring voice into decision-making, I have lots of experience with my survival brain.

When ThoughtExchange was just starting to grow and sell to more enterprise customers, we had a customer, Dessalen Wood, who was a VP Talent at the Canadian entertainment company Cineplex. She was a power user of our voice platform and was discovering all kinds of innovative places to leverage inclusion, including onboarding new leaders, national manager conversations, and L+D design. And more than a power user, she was, and is, an exceptional speaker and leader. I've had many opportunities to interact with her and see her speak and watch her in action. Cineplex was facing significant changes and I learned Dess was considering leaving and finding a new post.

We use messaging a lot in our internal company communication and I posted a quick message on Slack to see what people thought. My public message said something like this: "Hey team, I just learned one of our favorite customers, who is also an awesome leader and speaker, is potentially on the market. What are your thoughts on hiring her as our Chief People Officer?"

I immediately received a number of confirmatory messages, mostly from salespeople, who expressed their excitement and support. Many had either met her, or had heard about her, and were extremely supportive. After about five or six messages in the thread, there was a weird silence. My Spidey senses kicked in. Something didn't feel right about massive positivity and then total silence. So, I decided to launch an anonymous ThoughtExchange question into the same channel. Within a few minutes more than 70 people had joined the conversation. What was emerging you ask? More love and support? Nope. What was elevated was candor.

Thoughts that rose to the top were various flavors of things like: "Do we need a big corporate exec? Have you thought of whether she will fit in and do the work needed in a startup? Do we have the budget for a big corporate hire? Is this the wrong focus for us?" The concerns rolled in.

As an old-school facilitator and co-founder of a voice platform, of course I instantly opened my mind and my heart and accepted all of their feedback, grateful for their curiosity, and glad for the chance to more deeply evaluate this hire. That last sentence is a complete lie. My initial reaction was from my survival brain. I felt insulted! A little ticked off. Bemused. All sorts of self-preserving emotions flooded in as my initial reaction. As a CEO I should be trusted on issues of whether we had the budget! Or whether she would be a fit! How dare they have such strong opinions! They hadn't even met her and knew almost nothing about her!

You can see the humor in the whole thing in the last line. As I mentioned earlier, I don't consider myself a master of not being reactive, but I do think I have developed the memory muscle, when confronted by the unknown, to step back and not be overcome by the survival reaction. Rather than send a pissy note out to everyone I took some time and then came back to all of their thoughts, with the rest of my brain now thankfully intact. What was obvious the second time through was that... no one had met her and no one knew much about her!

What I knew about her was because of my experience with her directly. I realized, of course, no one else had been to the events where I had seen her speak and met with her on many occasions. So, when I asked for questions and important things to consider from everyone,

I got exactly that. Questions and important things to consider. Exactly what I had asked for.

After a few deep breaths, and enough time to consider the situation with my whole brain, I was able to empathize and feel gratitude. I recognized how I had failed to express my "Why" of Dess as our potential CPO ten times greater than the "What" of hiring her. My post in Slack was barely 1:1. Here was the ratio. Here's a person: She would be great. Not helpful. With that knowledge and clear articulations of excellent questions I was able to think through whether this was the right time and budget and person for this role. And after lots of discussion came to the conclusion that she was. It also meant that, when she started, she had a lot of clarification of her role across the company.

As a leader of a company that gathers unbiased truth from hundreds, I have hundreds of similar examples of leaders who felt confronted after seeing what everyone *actually* thinks. I've come to see that the larger the insight, the more open the leader has to be to receive it.

In fact, just the basic concept that, when you ask for feedback with names attached you get a small response, and when you use a tool to remove bias you get an enormous response, is confrontational. The questions then become, "What is lacking in me and my leadership that people feel afraid to speak up? Is using a tool to remove bias admitting I am a bad leader?" It's like counselling or coaching. "Does the fact I am working with someone else to become a better person make me a worse person?" The answer is, of course, No. The idea that you value ideas for their merit, not the identity of their sharer, is a sign of strength and even wisdom. The idea another human can counsel or coach you to help you grow is a sign of humility and openness. But that doesn't mean that you don't have to navigate the moments when your survival brain insists that you fight. When what you really need to do is sit down, take a breath, and let your whole mind and heart guide your next action.

When you encounter new ideas that make you feel upset, the most important thing is <u>not</u> to immediately ask yourself why. Instead, it's vital that, for a little while, you just do nothing at all. Turns out you're not facing a lion that will eat you. Breathe. If it's not a lion that will eat me . . . what is it? Let curiosity help you decide what to do next. It also leaves you open to listening and learning.

DEMONSTRATE LISTENING AND LEARNING

As is often the case in any process, the first step is the hardest. After you have moved past the self-defense mechanisms that inhibit learning, the remaining steps are somewhat easier. This is the core realm of leadership, and if you've read this far in this book I will assume you know a thing or two about being open to learning as a leader and demonstrating your ability to do so.

What I felt would be most helpful in this section is to make two distinctions. First, I want to distinguish listening and learning from their consequent actions. They are related but different.

There is a story about a person charged with an offence and they felt, beyond a doubt, that they were innocent. They got to have their day in court. The judge read the background on the case and immediately saw the error causing them to be incorrectly charged. Before the proceedings had even begun, the judge dismissed the case as there was enough evidence in the summary to release the person with a clear record. How did the person feel when the ruling was handed down? Elated? Relieved? Neither. They felt upset. They had carefully prepared their story and their argument and they had been extremely focused on their opportunity to share their voice. They were denied that opportunity. They felt frustrated, even though they had got exactly what they wanted. Ultimately, I imagine they were happier to be found not guilty, but that misses the point. People have a very real need to be heard and to have the listener demonstrate understanding. The actions the leader takes are important, but they are not everything. In fact, the actions that are taken can easily be misinterpreted when a demonstration of learning is absent.

With that distinction clear, it's easier to focus on a nearer-term success. What can I learn from the thoughts elevated in a scaled conversation? I don't need to agree or take action. The first step is to learn. With that lens the things you can learn include:

How people think and feel

What was surprising to you

What confirmed your assumptions

What language people use

What is not important

What is important

People trust leaders who have a disproportionate ability to learn and to demonstrate they have done so.

Imagine yourself on a different wilderness adventure again in yet another dangerous situation; this time you have a guide. Concerned about your safety and the safety of the group, you pull the guide aside and explain to them your experience on a different adventure in a similar place and the dangers that had lurked there. Consider what you need that guide to do for you to feel safe. They need to listen to you, understand you and demonstrate that they have done so. If they do that, then they gain your trust. When they make their next decisions, you feel they are informed and have the best chance to keep everyone safe. If they don't give you that chance to express yourself, and don't demonstrate their understanding, how do you feel? Anxious. Worried the guide is lacking critical information. You might even feel suddenly responsible for the lives of the people on the trip, even though you are not the guide yourself, and that could result in all sorts of behaviors—from you and the others in the group. The more the guide demonstrates proficiency and the ability to take on ideas, the more you trust them.

The same can be applied to medical professionals looking after your health. The more they are willing to listen, and not dismiss your input about your body and your particular situation, the more you trust their recommendations and actions. The less they appear to be listening, the more anxious you become that you are being misunderstood, and potentially misdiagnosed.

The key with the adventure guide and the medical professional is that, whether they appear to be listening or not, they could both be taking in relevant data from their surroundings, and your input, and they could then be recommending you take exactly the correct actions. But, without the trust that results from them listening, and demonstrating that they have done so, you might not follow them. You might be tempted to try other routes, other solutions, other leaders. As trust is built through demonstrated listening and learning, however, you, in turn, come to trust them. And trust is fast. You learn what input might be helpful, and when they likely have enough information to make a decision, and move quick.

Scaling conversations using technology is a powerful opportunity to build this kind of trust at scale. Responding back to people about what you have learned is suddenly possible across hundreds, and even thousands, of people as you elevate what matters most and demonstrate what you have learned or are learning before you take any actions.

The second distinction is between understanding and agreeing. While we may aspire to understand as many people as possible, it is, of course, not possible to agree with everyone. But that's OK. Accessing the un-biased voice of many gives you enormous opportunities to learn and understand where people are coming from. It also gives you a great opportunity to agree or disagree with a more complete awareness. There is a common, outdated misconception about what people think in decision making. It is this: Everyone wants things their way. That's simply not true. What is truer is that many, and even most, people understand they are part of a larger complex system in which many people have many different needs. They understand things can't necessarily go their way all the time. Or even much of the time. Call me an optimist, but in general most people are mostly reasonable. There are people with extreme viewpoints and extreme needs, but the reason we call them extreme is simply because they are far from the center. And the center is reasonable. As soon as everyone is unreasonable, the extreme viewpoints will be the reasonable ones.

"With great power comes great responsibility." This saying is not outdated or a misconception. Once you have mastered the rest of this book to attain conversations at scale you do have a great responsibility to try to understand people. And here is where the distinction comes in. You don't have an extreme responsibility to agree with everyone. The concept of collective intelligence is not a magical mysterious aspect of humanity. It is simply the notion that a group of people is often smarter than an expert on a subject. And, if that subject is "How the group feels about change" you can tap into the collective feeling about what people believe to be true. That doesn't make it true.

Early on, as a startup with only 30 or 40 ThoughtExchange staff, we scaled a conversation about what people believed to be our best strategy for the next year. We had one target market segment we focused 50% of our time on and we spread the rest of our time and effort on other markets and customers. Our staff, at that point, felt strongly that 50% of our time on only one type of customer was wrong; instead, we needed to focus on going as broad as we could, targeting all kinds of different sectors and verticals. Anyone familiar with *Crossing the Chasm* or startup strategy will see the challenge with this. In the early days it is critical to focus on solving one problem deeply before you then head on to serve other segments. In the automotive industry getting this wrong would be creating a car brand that promises luxury, economy, four by four capability, city class, racing ability, environmental friendliness, family and individual focus that targets both wealthy and low-income individuals. Completely impossible. So, you need to segment.

What was true for our company in that moment was that we needed to all come together and first get really excited about the broad applicability of an inclusive voice platform across all industries. We then needed to educate everyone on the importance of growing with focus before we expand. People wanted to be heard on the fact that we had a much broader potential than the narrow focus we took initially. It was important to hear from everyone on that. And it was also critical I didn't agree with them.

This is a hard skill, but the good news is that prioritized voice gathered during a scaled conversation is very often helpful and contains excellent recommendations for actions. It is normally possible to both learn and agree. But what is important is that those two things are different and you acknowledge that.

By distinguishing between what it means to learn and understand, and what it means to agree and take action, you can communicate your educational journey and unlock the trust you need to take the next step.

Adopt Language

This one is quite simple, and what is most important about adopting language is to recognize the power of it that is hiding in plain sight. The words you use, or assume others use in the same way, matter. Let me start with an example.

A large public school system was trying to learn why their community had not supported their long-range facility plans. The community needed to vote to approve the funding for the plan and for many years they had not. Time after time a plan was put to the community to vote on and it failed to get approval. The leadership was very clear on the needs of their schools and students, but the community didn't agree.

As part of their process, they decided to scale a conversation to include thousands of people. They learned many things from the usually unheard majority and one aspect really stood out. The district had a plan to upgrade old schools built in the 1940s and '50s by rebuilding them on the same site where they stood. When they scaled a conversation with the community, they heard something that was confusing at first. People articulated frustration that the school was investing taxpayers' money in renovating schools. They did not approve of that strategy. But, interestingly enough, because it was a conversation they were able to learn that those same people very much supported and agreed with the idea of building a new school on the original site, rather than renovate the old building. Anything to do with a new building resonated, while the idea of renovation did not. Here's the wild part: Those were both the exact same idea. The district wanted to rebuild on site and their communications called that renovation. The community associated renovation with some sort of homebuilding trauma they had all experienced, or they didn't see its value: Something more ambitious was needed.

The leadership instantly came to recognize that they needed to adopt the language of building new on site and to clarify their intent. This was one of many critical steps that needed to happen to achieve their goal of gaining support, which they achieved in the following months.

Adopting language is powerful and is also grounded in respect. As a leader of diverse people with different backgrounds and methods of communication it is important to learn how to adopt language and clarify your own intentions at scale. Oftentimes in a conversation, two extremely similar thoughts, with similar intentions, will be perceived very differently due to a nuance of language. By being curious about that difference you can learn a great deal about language and how to communicate. Maybe, more importantly, you can learn about your own privilege and the lens you bring to any issue.

The root of this idea is a concept I learned from Jessie Hutton Nelson, an inclusion facilitator, consultant and an exceptional source of knowledge you can learn about on kithandcommon.ca.

Jessie says the distinction is between the golden rule and the platinum rule.

The golden rule is known by one and all. It's a principle. Treat others as you want to be treated. That's a pretty great rule. But consider what Jessie described to ThoughtExchange during a training session as the platinum rule: Treat others as <u>they</u> want to be treated.

It turns out that some people might not want to be treated, or to communicate with you, in the same way you would expect or hope. People have their own history, context and culture. Rather than expect them all to conform, we can do our best to communicate and relate to others in a way that they would want.

As you work to understand, communicate and take action on the prioritized voice of hundreds or thousands consider it a platinum opportunity to learn how to communicate with people as they would like.

The core challenge we need to get over, in our society, is to acknowledge our poor history of practicing the platinum rule. As a privileged white male, with colonizing ancestors who recently sought to destroy the language and culture of the indigenous people, who had flourishing languages and societies on the unceded land where I and fellow North Americans now live, work and play, it is important to recognize that respecting people and adopting their language in an effort to understand them, and best meet their needs because you assume they are worthy of your trust and support, was not historically...common. The opposite is our history. Disrespect, and the intentional division—and in many cases destruction—of people who think and communicate differently, is our observable pattern as humans. The result is, divided people and a rapid destruction of critical life systems. Dismantling the short-sighted, fear-based systems that have created so much harm is critical. Understanding the mechanisms to do that in your day-to-day communication is one way you can contribute.

On its surface adopting language is a way to influence people. On a deeper level it is a way to more deeply understand and serve them.

We've now arrived at the final step of what you need to do to synthesize scaled conversation: Commit to action.

Commit to Action (Even If the Action Is to Take None)

Though learning, understanding, and adopting language are essential and extremely valuable, the most important synthesis of results are the actions you take as a result of what you have learned. Even when that action is to take no action. I'll explain.

At the beginning of this book, I talked about earning leadership capital and working with the hierarchy of questions to help you generate the insights and buy-in you need to deliver on the mission of your organization. Throughout the book I've attempted to explain why, and how, you can do that by including hundreds or even thousands of people you lead in decisions that affect them. Now, let's consider what this looks like in action by considering the actions that result from each level of the scaled-conversation hierarchy: Safety, structure, connection, alignment, culture, vision, and transformation.

Safety

Safety conversations are mostly about accessing concerns, empathy, and shared understanding. Such conversations primarily require clarification and a demonstration of listening. Typically, the actions that need to be taken when safety is lacking are emotionally based. Trying to fix how someone is feeling by immediately making a change in their environment very seldom works. Appropriate responses to safety conversations are often: Commitment to further conversation; commitment to providing clarity on anything ambiguous or misunderstood; and a commitment to bringing in experts and resources to help with challenges. Because lack of safety leads to low trust, any actions that are taken in such a context won't be effective: Establishing trust is paramount. This requires validation and a fundamental and renewed sense of communication.

Structure

Actions taken in conversations about structure can be more tangible. You've asked the question about what is working well and what could be improved so now it is time to categorize the top-rated responses into action buckets.

Some helpful structure buckets are:

Already doing (Existing actions that need communications)
Action immediately (Low-hanging fruit)
Medium-term action (On the roadmap in the near future)

Long-term action (Requires education and agreement but agreeable in the long-term)

Needs investigation (Not enough understanding to take action or not take action)

Not actioning (Not doing for reasons you explain)

By placing recommendations into these buckets and using the margarita thoughts in the conversation you have both prioritization and a communication tool to help explain how input has affected decision-making.

Connection

Connection actions are about what "We" can do together. Remember, the essence of connection questions is about storytelling. And since the stories themselves hold the power, the main way to action these exchanges is to focus on the method of dissemination of those stories.

The first and most simple way is to create a communication that simply shares the top 20 insights or stories from the group and to highlight them as the stories found to be important. Stories about overcoming challenges, learning important lessons, recognizing the hard work of others, etc., all need to be shared publicly for their effect to be "actioned."

One way we do this at ThoughtExchange is to host a monthly meeting where we scale a conversation to surface the top, important stories from all around the company. These can be internal or external stories and contain one daunting but important element. The process of sharing story subjects, and rating stories by which ones you most want to hear, is confidential. However, we also request that those who shared the top story subjects take five minutes to tell their story live to everyone on the video call. The question we ask monthly is: What story would we all benefit from hearing right now? And, if your story comes to the top please be willing to share it!

This storytelling process creates both insight and a strong sense of unity as the tales we most want to hear get shared from sometimes surprising corners of the company. The meeting is recorded and accessible afterward to everyone who wasn't at the meeting.

There are many ways to disseminate stories once they've been gathered; the most important thing is that you do it. Stories are extremely powerful in the right context and told to the right people.

Alignment

Alignment actions are about continuous improvement. The questions here seek to optimize a team that is connected and moving forward. The same action buckets apply from the Structure level and are perhaps even more important since there will likely be many more small actions that can make a big difference.

In this category I have seen questions sent by sales leaders to improve the sales process of underperforming teams that generate dozens of useful suggestions to increase revenue.

I've seen leaders who are crafting $400 million facility improvement plans scale conversations on how the project can be improved before putting it on a ballot for a bond approval vote. The actions are about project prioritization, language changes, locations of new buildings, etc. Changes in plans are communicated prior to any election.

I've also seen sales departments ask for additional resources and competitive intelligence professionals ask where their assets are lacking.

Finally, I've seen several large school districts scale conversations about changing their start times. More often than not the resulting action is to do nothing after they learn that people are generally happy with the status quo while, in fact, a loud minority was insisting that "Everyone wants the start times to change." Once it is established that the majority are happy, it's easy to do nothing at all. The action of deliberately not taking action is the result of a conversation, not of not wanting to have a conversation.

In all of these cases the actions are obvious because the need was clear: The question was candid and the leader nailed the hierarchy.

When alignment questions are nailed, there is no burden to actioning results. Instead, it feels like a superpower of understanding what people need, which facilitates a process of ruthlessly prioritizing the highest return actions to help your organization move forward.

Culture

Culture conversations are about making the best of your organization observable. As with connection questions, the critical aspect of culture questions is to make the results available, and refer to them often.

Another less obvious aspect of culture-talk is that the conversation itself is the dissemination of the results. Asking people to share and rate thoughts about what makes their organization special; What makes how they work together unique; What actions exemplify the best of their shared culture, etc., allows them to experience each other's thinking. In the context of culture, often the path is more important than the goal.

It is still important to share results. But the true goal is to have those cultural conversations as often as you can, which requires staying quite high up on the scaled conversations hierarchy through intentional effort.

Vision

Vision questions are about imagining a future together. Organizationally, they are so high up the scaled conversations hierarchy that they are rare. Or at least they should be if you are really listening.

Actioning vision on a long-term basis is really about the long-term commitment to the process of visioning and communicating that vision succinctly, with a stated timeline for revision. Organizations now generally have three- or five-year strategic plans with vision exercises taking place in coordination with that effort. Best practice is to disseminate a one-page document that distills the results of your vision conversations in pithy, relatable terms. The actions "therefore" are related to the creation and updating of these vision processes and the associated communications.

That said, another type is near-term visioning. After earning the right to visualize the future, on sharing what makes the present successful, it's possible to vision at team level. Questions such as this are more immediately actionable: What will we be doing by the end of this year that will demonstrate we are successful? The resulting actions are to share progress and to joyfully iterate as new information becomes available. In the realm of vision there is by its nature a lot of unknowns so actions are about communicating as the future becomes the present. A practical example of this is to have a working session to revisit previous visioning conversation results and to discuss successes and challenges with the intent to establish the next vision.

One way we have actioned this at ThoughtExchange is when we shared a slideshow, set to music, of all the things we had hoped the year to be as we collectively realized just how many of our goals had been achieved. This slideshow created a strong sense of accomplishment and a desire to bravely vision again.

Transformation

> "If you want to build a ship, don't drum up the men to gather wood, divide the work, and give orders. Instead, teach them to yearn for the vast and endless sea."
> —Antoine De Saint-Exupery, author of *The Little Prince*

Transformation is about radical and complete change. Actioning conversations about transformation creates a common yearning for a better reality, without filling in the mundane requirements of reality. It's like a wild prototype car of the future made of fictional materials achieving unrealistic things. It's a future in which racism is finally completely dismantled. The point is to generate a sense of possibility which is sufficiently vague that your inner skeptic can't come in and ruin the transformative nature of the conversation by dragging it into the realm of continuous improvement.

The actions, then, are to ensure the point of the conversation is not to create near-term actions. Any near-term actions that result from a transformative conversation are false.

The Blackfoot taught that the top of the hierarchy is the realm of generations in the future. Multi-generational sustainability is a transformation since currently the future is anything but.

In a well-known spiritual story, a stonecutter is asked: "What are you doing?" To which the stonecutter replied: "I'm cutting this piece of stone and I look forward to getting it cut so I can go home." A second stonecutter cutting a similar piece of rock nearby is asked: "What are you doing?" The response was different: "I'm building a wall and I look forward to when it is complete in a few months so I can take a vacation." A third stonecutter nearby is asked: "What are you doing?" Their answer was different than either of the first two. "Me? I am a cathedral builder building a great cathedral in the service of God."

Taking action of transformation is keeping the purpose of your effort in the hearts and minds of people by reminding them that the most important work can never be achieved in the span of a single lifetime. If you are working on something you know can undoubtedly be finished during your time on earth, you are not thinking big enough. You are not thinking transformationally.

By thinking about things in the realm of transformation across a span of space and time greater than your lifetime you are adding purpose to every small step you take in the meantime as you tackle the next problem and navigate change.

In summary, the way you synthesize results of scaled conversations is not as simple as applying a cookie-cutter approach to all situations. Instead, it is the work of unifying the voice of your organizations with your efforts to lead it. If it is done well there is little or no gap between what you feel are your ideas and what the ideas of "your people" are. Your ideas are instead formed by scaling conversations with your employees, customers and community and your actions are the results of a healthy relationship with the people you are meant to lead and to serve.

CHAPTER 11

Scaling Conversations in Action: Diversity, Inclusion, Mental Health, Equity

N ow that we've gone through how to scale conversations by meeting people where they are at, asking great questions and overcoming obstacles to synthesize and disseminate results, only one thing is left: Institutionalizing it. And by that I mean finding the opportunities in your organization to operationalize and leverage the unbiased voices of your employees, customers and community to unify their effort with your leadership on a regular cadence. No problem. With great power comes great responsibility and this final section is about how and when conversations can be leveraged to solve critical problems facing organizations and societies.

For the purposes of this book and this chapter I have focused on four areas: Diversity, Inclusion, Equity, and Mental Health. To different leaders these topics could mean different things. For example, if you are leading a sales team, leveraging diversity means exceeding your sales targets by increasing the performance of your team by creating systems to access the breakthrough thinking of diverse people. If you are a school superintendent, leveraging diversity is about dismantling systemic racism, addressing poverty, respecting cultures as you work to equitably optimize learning outcomes for all kids regardless of the systems that have been in their way in the past.

Though the challenges are different, in the context of scaling conversations, the underpinnings of the initiatives are the same. Diversity is about successfully increasing the range of people and ideas your teams interact with. Inclusion is about intentionally leveraging the value of diversity by eliminating bias as you surface insight from as many people as possible on all problems you face. Mental health is about recognizing all people as people with emotional needs that need to be validated for them to contribute to your shared mission. Equity is about revising policy and practices to ensure your organization is continually learning from the people you are trying to create equitable opportunities for, and who are each uniquely affected by the decisions being made about them.

Let's get into each one.

Diversity

Diversity is very simply defined as a range of different things. When it comes to talking about diversity in organizations than range relates to skin color, gender, sexuality, the way we think, cultural backgrounds, personality types, etc.

In relation to scaling conversations, it seems efforts to increase organizational diversity fit into two buckets, one more obvious that the other. Let's start with the more obvious one: Respect. At a fundamental level each of us has the right to be respected and that respect should in no way diminish due to the things that make us different. Our skin color, heritage, gender, sexual orientation, etc., shouldn't affect how others think about our ability to contribute to creating value in any organization. This should be self-evident in 2021, but painfully, it is often not. Tackling this aspect of diversity is critical and success in setting a foundation of respect creates all kinds of positive outcomes as people feel safe and motivated to contribute in a positive and intentionally diverse environment.

The second bucket in the effort to increase organizational diversity is less obvious but perhaps more important to the context of this book: Leverage. In this case I am defining leverage as the ability to use something to its maximum advantage. Often diversity is thought of primarily as a correct thing to do regardless of its ability to maximize anything. Respect is a right and it should be extended despite leverage. That said, humans are historically not that great at doing things because of the basic rights of others or of the planet. Producing and driving electric cars has been the right thing to do for a long time but with vested interests in fossil fuel vehicles hindering progress and without personal economic equations—aka, what's in it for me?—they have been slow to get produced and consumed in volume. Now that they are marketable, less expensive, accelerate faster, have better stereos and just may be a small part of helping us avoid a planetary catastrophe (fingers crossed), they are getting adopted faster. Once they are simply more profitable to sell and less expensive to purchase and operate than the competing gas versions, they will dominate the highways. The technology is very close to making this possible. Simple economics drives so much of human behavior.

When it comes to getting people to activate greater diversity in their organizations, the economics are not something we need to wait for as the technology develops. The economics are already here, just not completely obvious or understood. Yet. Let's take the "guessing the weight of a ox" story reported in 1907 by the famous statistician Sir Francis Galton and made famous by all sorts of people such as James Suroweki in *The Wisdom of Crowds*, NPR in their "weight of a cow experiment and even in National Geographic where they extended the concept to report on how groups of animals are more intelligent, by a long shot, than individual animals.[1]

In all of these studies it shows that, when it comes to determining the measurable gravitational effect of a bovine, crowds outperform experts as long as you have many guesses and a manner for aggregating them. But one aspect is often mentioned but seldom emphasized. As Suroweki outlines in his critical components for crowd wisdom, it turns out a crowd of similar experts actually gets outperformed by a diverse crowd containing experts and non-experts. In this experiment re-run by NPR where 17,000 people helped guess the weight of a cow, and came within 50 pounds, it was shown that the self-described experts were not as correct alone without adding the guesses of the nonexperts.[2] Experts were off by 6% versus the 5% error bar of the diverse crowd. Bingo.

The phenomenon here is not that diverse contributors necessarily have better ideas or intuition. They may or may not. The explanation is that greater diversity causes a greater range of guesses and, critically, a lesser chance of everyone getting misled by a shared bias. Shared bias is scary and results in things like the earth obviously rotating around the sun. Minimizing the negative effects of bias thanks to diversity can do much more than guess the weight of a cow. Think: Achieve market dominance with a new product, create a safer workplace, pass a critical referendum. And it's proven.

In organizations, hiring and involving people with diverse perspectives will make the group smarter and more innovative. According to HBR's 2018 article "How and Where Diversity Drives Financial Performance" by Rocio Lorenzo and Martin Reeves, companies with higher-than-average diversity also have 19% higher innovation revenue. Simple. In a 2015 McKinsey article entitled "Why Diversity Matters," Vivian Hunt, Dennis Layton, and Sara Prince reported that the most ethnically diverse companies are 35% more likely to surpass their peers and gender-diverse companies are 15% more likely. Obvious. Do both.

Evidence of the competitive advantages of diversity is increasing as more and more companies achieve success in this area and measure the outcome. The good news is that if you're paying attention, the economics of leveraging diversity is so obvious that organizations not working to achieve more diversity are arguably negligent in terms of their responsibilities to their shareholders and/or stakeholders. So, the decision to attempt to become more diverse is an easy one.

That said, achieving and activating more diversity is one of those things that is simple but not easy. Every organization has its own set of challenges that need to be addressed in order to succeed and every organization is at a different place in creating or achieving their diversity goals.

The following question set is designed to meet your organization where they are at when it comes to diversity. This area of inquiry is gaining traction but is emotional and provocative so starting at the bottom of the scaled conversations hierarchy (safety) and preparing for reactive responses and deep leader learning is really important. By actively asking people to share concerns about the current state you open the door to exploring issues higher up the hierarchy. With this subject in particular skipping over the base level of security will have potentially harmful effects. Handle with care and work with experts to understand results.

Diversity

Safety: What is on your hearts and minds about diversity in our organization?

Structure: What are some systems and structures we could consider to improve in the area of diversity?

Connection: What can we all do together to help ensure we are respecting and leveraging the power of diversity in our organization?

Alignment: What advice do you have for things we can do to improve in respect to hiring and retaining excellent diverse team members?

Culture: What are some of the best examples of how we have respected and leveraged diversity in our organization in the past?

Vision: Imagine it's two years from now and we are doing an incredible job respecting and leveraging the power diversity in our organization. What sort of things are we doing to create this success?

Transformation: What will be possible in the future regarding diversity in our organization?

INCLUSION

Which came first, the chicken or the egg? When you are prioritizing organizational development, which comes first, diversity or inclusion? At first glance there is no easy answer. Or more simply, no answer. Thinking a bit more deeply, it turns out there is an answer to both.

Understanding evolution means you understand species evolve over time and something that wasn't really a chicken laid an egg containing what turned out to be, as a mutation or a next step forward, a thing we call a chicken. And that chicken survived. Maybe because of its pecking power. Who knows? But the egg came first. And without the egg there was no container for the chicken to be successful within.

That explanation is admittedly pseudo-science at best, but is meant to drive home a point: Similar to that order, diversity and inclusion also have a logical progression. The best way to describe it is pseudo-math.

In the last section on diversity I argued, hopefully successfully, that increasing diversity has easy-to-calculate ROI. More diversity equals better. Easy. There's a catch though, which is related to why diversity is still slow to catch on despite obvious advantages. It requires delving further into diversity before we can have a discussion on inclusion.

Let's take three different shapes representing three different (diverse) types of people:

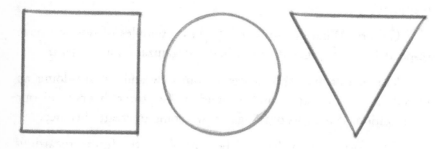

Say each of these shapes has a total surface area of 10 and therefore, for the sake of argument, each person can contribute 10 diversity points. Three different shapes × 10 = 30 total available diversity points. And also for the sake of argument around diversity, imagine that every time you just have another similar person, or square on the left, you don't get any increase in diversity points. So, you can add 20 "squares" together and you still only get a total of 10 diversity points. Making sense? More people exactly like you don't add up.

Overall, you want to increase the diversity of your shapes so you can increase the total surface area and therefore your diversity points.

The first thought is to just add lots of different shapes/people and, *voila*, you get lots of diversity points. Yet to achieve effectiveness around diversity, the people have to work together. They have to hear one another's ideas and be willing to learn how one another adds value to the problems everyone is trying to solve together. Even when their contributions are wrong, perhaps they are wrong in interesting ways. Like the people guessing the weight of a cow. Maybe someone guesses ridiculously low, say 500 pounds when the cow is actually 1,800 pounds, because the cow, to them, looks skinny. Well, that's wrong but it helps the average get closer to the truth because though it is a 2,000-pound animal, it is, in fact, skinny for a cow. So, the notion of "skinny" helped though the number was wildly wrong.

The problem with diversity is that diverse people, unaided, don't necessarily know how to gather the best thinking of one another. Bias creeps in. Communication challenges emerge. A 500-pound cow? You know nothing about cows! Idiot. That thing has to be at least 2,000 pounds. Any other people with stupid ideas? So, the three shapes above, in practice, look more like this:

And, as diverse people attempt to add value independently, it turns out the net gain is actually only the spot where they are already similar. Where they intersect.

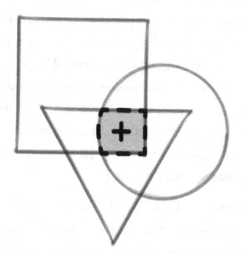

Diverse people working together without tools to augment bias and INCLUDE the best thinking of one another actually reduce their effectiveness and, instead of a net gain of 30, you get the overlapping area that amounts to about... two.

Picture three very different people working on a project with no inspiration or training to work together. The result is the opposite of optimal. Those three people work worse together than they would have apart. You'd be better off just hiring three similar people, and getting the net diversity score of 10, than fall back to a sum of three.

But there's hope.

A foundation of inclusion is critical. People need to understand how to engage with the essence of ideas instead of the people who share them. They must acknowledge and be willing to augment their biases. They need to be able to approach one another with candor and, more importantly, extraordinary respect, to actualize the value of diversity.

Only when everyone learns how to include one another utilizing technology along with enhanced self-reflection and communication skills can diversity thrive.

So, inclusion has to come first. It's the egg. The essential container of change if you will. If your organization doesn't fundamentally value and practice inclusion you can have all the diversity you want and the result is only the tiny intersection in the middle.

But by practicing inclusion AND increasing diversity, you get the value of all of the areas EXCEPT the areas where people intersect. While it's great to be in a meeting where people think like you and agree with you and support you, ultimately, it's not. It turns out it is much more satisfying to interact with people and ideas that help you grow as you accept and challenge one another.

Acknowledgement that you need to prioritize inclusion is only a step though. Opening conversations about it is an entirely different thing.

I remember as a kid sitting alone in a cabin at Educo Adventure School, my favorite place on earth as a young teenager, while a group of slightly older people gathered down by the lake by a fire. I didn't feel included. I hated that place that day. It was my favorite place and they were all people I admired. But the feeling of being on the outside was so strong that it triggered my survival instinct to flee. As an adult I'm pretty sure if I had just walked down there I would have been invited and included. But I had a fear, rational or not, that if I walked up someone would tell me to go away. There I was, mad at a group of people for something they hadn't done and would likely never do. But that didn't matter. I was upset and I never did join them. I fell asleep alone.

Thinking back to that time I recognize two opposing truths. The first is it was my responsibility to get over my irrational fear and to just go and join the group. Get out of my comfort zone. Be brave. Including myself was the key element to ensuring I was inside the circle and not on the outside. At the same time, I had some barriers in my mind: I was younger than everyone, I was stuck in a bad place, so I didn't. The other truth is that the group needed to reach out to me and notice I wasn't included. I was the only one alone and someone needed to notice that and reach out. Without someone on the inside of the circle actively inviting me to cross the threshold from out to in, I wasn't capable of doing it by myself. Even if someone had simply called for me I would have likely come, maybe pretending I had been too busy to just join earlier.

Balancing the reality that individuals and groups are both responsible for inclusion is really important. People need to want to be included and they need to believe in their ability to add value. Groups need to want to include everyone and therefore need to ask themselves about who is not in the circle and how can that change.

And while we do this, we need to recognize inclusion is right in the middle of what makes us human. It is emotional, and perhaps even more than emotional, it is instinct. Animals need to stick with the herd. People don't want to be on the outside of the community or tribe. By nature. Not that long ago it meant life or death.

So, dealing with inclusion as it relates to ourselves and others is often dealing with rawness and unexpected reactivity. As long as we recognize that going in, we can prepare to get more related with one another so we can hear one another and work to remove the barriers and systems that exclude.

This question set on inclusion can set a path for transforming your organization. At the same time, be warned, this topic is loaded and requires care and a massive willingness to be open to learning on behalf of the leaders.

Inclusion

Safety: What's in your hearts and minds about inclusion in our company?

Structure: What are some decisions or changes we are making where we could include more voices and candor?

Connection: What can we all do together to improve how we include one another in our organization?

Alignment: What advice do you have for things we can do to improve how we include voices and ideas across teams in our organization?

Culture: What are some of the best examples of how we have included diverse voices and ideas in the past?

Vision: Imagine it's the future and we are doing an excellent job of including all voices and ideas in our organization. What sorts of things are we doing to create this success?

Transformation: What is possible now that wasn't possible before regarding including voices and ideas in our organization?

MENTAL HEALTH

I'm in my mid-twenties and I am storming breathlessly into a doctors' clinic in a mall in North Vancouver. I stumble past the reception and force my way into an already occupied doctor's office.

"Someone help me, I'm dying," I exclaim and collapse on the floor. The patient in the room must have left. I didn't notice.

The doctor assessed me on the floor with his or her stethoscope (I can't remember their face or gender).

"What's wrong?" the doctor asked.

"I don't know, I think I'm having some sort of massive heart attack and I can't breathe," I replied, more than a little panicked.

Then the doctor asked what seemed like a completely unrelated and bizarre question: "Has someone close to you had a massive heart attack recently?"

I looked up. "Actually...yes." I was stalled in time by the question. "My dad died of one recently."

"That makes sense," said the doctor. "Your heart rate is fine, your breathing is good and you seem to be in excellent health. You are experiencing a panic attack. Have you heard of panic attacks before?"

"No," I replied.

"You are safe, you aren't having a heart attack and this will soon pass. I'm going to give you an Ativan. You lie down for a few minutes and I'll come explain what happened."

That was my experiential crash course in mental health.

In my mid-twenties my father passed away unexpectedly of a massive heart attack. He was in his 50s. Prior to that experience my life had had ups and downs, all within a relatively small range. His death was my first major down.

After that dramatic entry into the world of panic attacks I spent the better part of the next year-and-a-half riding a bit of a hellish wave. That first panic attack sparked an ongoing series of panic attacks that would come while I slept, while I drove over bridges, while I was out to lunch with friends. And, being armed with the fact that I wasn't actually dying wasn't all that helpful when every day I very literally felt like I was.

My journey with anxiety and mental health challenges led me through all sorts of doctors, who told me I had all sorts of disorders and allergies and prescribed me all sorts of drugs, ranging from acid reflux to antidepressants to sleeping pills. The happy ending is, after spending too many hours lying on the cold floor of private and public bathrooms, and often sprinting through the park at 2:00 am trying to outrun myself, I found resolution and closure with my Dad's shocking passing through meditation, and to some degree, through the passage of time. The anxiety released its grip and I have been free of full-on panic attacks since; though many of the smaller symptoms can still surface under stress.

The reason I share that story is actually about what happened next. When I first had panic attacks, I had never heard of such a thing. While I was experiencing them I was too ashamed to tell anyone but my closest friends and family what was happening. Once panic released its grip, I started to tell people what had happened to me and I shared stories about how my life was thrown completely off course for a very long time due to mental health and grieving.

The response from people I shared this story with was surprising at first, and then soon predictable:

"I've had that too."
"I've gone to the ER too."
"I've called an ambulance."
"I have those often still but don't tell anyone."
"My sister has those I think."

And I would ask all the people I talked to: "Did you know about them before you experienced one?"

Invariably: "No."

That was about 17 years ago, and the world has changed a fair bit around this issue. Overall, there is a lot more awareness about anxiety and I think/hope a lot more people who experience a panic attack will have at least heard of such a thing prior to having that lovely pretend glove of death wrapped around their poor throats.

But awareness in general doesn't change one fundamental fact: Challenges with mental health are everywhere. I am a CEO of a successful software company and I have always been an entrepreneur and someone you'd describe as confident and fortunate. I've never experienced war or violence or discrimination. Quite the opposite: I have experienced white privilege in a democratic country and was blessed with the strong foundation of growing up in a loving and inclusive home in a small town. Prior to experiencing a few years of hell, I would have guessed I was the "last sort of person" to struggle with mental health.

Of course, now I understand this all very differently. It turns out many in my extended family, past and present, struggle with various mental health challenges and take a number of different approaches to dealing with them. By sharing my story, I learned that many of my friends, colleagues, even strangers, have had similar experiences.

Mental health is a combination of chemistry and past life experience, and while I am a student of one kind of anxiety, I don't profess to be any kind of expert. What I do know is that talking about my struggles is therapeutic for me and has been helpful for others. Being willing to share what scared me, and what fears I still have, is helpful. It's vitally important. And while we spend a lot of time thinking about what we need to "do," how we feel and what we are afraid of needs to be discussed at scale. And it requires safety and compassion to do so.

Not long ago it would have seemed crazy for leaders to ask about the mental state of employees, customers, and community members. That was supposed to be "at home" stuff you don't bring to your organization. Now it seems crazy NOT to. Your employees, customers, and community are experiencing all sorts of things and could literally be in any state of mind and struggling with any sort of mental challenge. To be sure, this is not group therapy led by amateurs. I don't mean you should ask about what personal trauma may be part of what might be ailing someone.

What I do think is important is finding ways to check in with people and scale conversations about how people are feeling and what sort of support they might need to be their best. Why? Because it is critical for people to understand they are not alone. They are not broken because they are afraid or overwhelmed during good times and hard times. Simply getting people to share their fears, concerns, challenges is valuable by itself. Getting them to consider and empathize with thoughts shared by other people in similar roles, who have similar fears, concerns and challenges, is gold.

The overall effect of connecting with people you identify with about fears and concerns in an open and safe way is relieving. Knowing you are not alone allows you to reconnect with your feelings and, often, to move past them.

While the overall topic is complex and loaded, the mechanism of hosting a conversation about how people are feeling is surprisingly simple. You know how to do it. Picture yourself checking in with a good friend in the middle of the COVID-19 pandemic. What sort of language do you use? What is the purpose of the questions you ask? These are actually simple things to consider. You ask how they're feeling. You ask what concerns they have or what challenges they are facing. You ask how you can help. Within the context of safety and care that friend is free to answer however they wish and they'll feel better for it. And chances are they'll ask you those same questions back and as you share your thoughts you'll both feel closer. Maybe you find something you can do to help, an action you can take. Maybe you just talk and listen and that's enough.

During the early days of the pandemic many organizations we work with took inspirational approaches to meeting people where they are at. A massive software company asked all of their sales reps about resources they needed to attain to be successful in the new environment. They uncovered gaps in tools, hopes of team members and frustrations that needed to be considered.

A statewide association of School Superintendents hosted video conferences with hundreds of leaders. They opened the session by asking "What is on your hearts and minds as a Superintendent right now? The results were extremely powerful. Fears, frustrations, hopes and challenges were all shared. After that question they asked another: What is a story this group most needs to hear right now? And if your story comes to the top, please be willing to briefly share it to the whole group." Incredible stories surfaced and leaders took turns telling moving accounts of challenges and personal anguish and even personal transformation inspired by their largest professional challenges. It was a forum where leaders felt safe to share their hearts and minds and, critically, to remember that they were not alone.

A manufacturing company took on another angle with their employees. With the spread of COVID-19 accelerating in their area over the summer it became obvious that remote work would continue and those with school-aged children would not have their children back in classes in the fall. They invited parents to join an online meeting where they first asked everyone: "What's in your hearts and minds with children not returning to school in the Fall?" Nearly 100 people shared concerns and fears. After the leader addressed the top thoughts they moved up the hierarchy and asked: "What are some structures and processes that might need to be addressed to support our staff with kids at home?" Almost 200 thoughts were rated 2,000 times in a few minutes. Advice, ideas, comments arose, and the leaders spoke with care to what emerged and promised action. Just as importantly, the group provided incredible feedback to the leader in the group chat:

> "It was wonderful to not feel alone"
> "Thank you for hearing our voices"
> "It's wonderful to see our leaders show how much they care"
> "This is a great example of how (our company) is invested in our employees"

As we navigate through pandemics and uprisings and the next industrial revolution with people working remotely in many languages from all around the world, it has become a business imperative to be willing to open conversations about how people are feeling, the challenges they are experiencing and the need to focus on our mental health.

Using the safety of a conversation platform to scale, you can have conversations to help uncover challenges and ensure people don't feel alone. In turn, people feel free to share concerns that will, in turn, allow them to move up the scaled conversations hierarchy and share their creativity and passion.

Mental Health

Safety: What's on the top of your hearts and minds right now?

Structure: What structures or processes might need to be addressed as we navigate challenges in the months to come?

Connection: What can we all do together to ensure we are supporting one another to their best as we navigate challenges?

Alignment: What advice do you have for things we can do to improve how our organization supports you?

Culture: What are some great examples of how we are navigating challenges right now?

Vision: Imagine it's the future and we are doing an excellent job of supporting everyone's mental health. What sort of things are we doing to create this success?

Transformation: What will be possible in the future regarding mental health and wellness?

EQUITY

Equity is the quality of being fair. More than equality, equity speaks to the need for leaders to ensure they have created an environment where everyone has a chance to succeed and contribute to that success regardless of what systemic issues may be in the way of them accessing the same opportunity as others. You've probably seen a version of two pictures of people standing on crates trying to see over a fence:

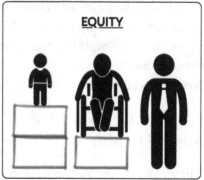

Liberation and social justice is removing the fence itself, and while we all work to dismantle the systems that make it necessary to augment the bias-reducing abilities of humans and to keep convincing people of the more than obvious power of inclusion and diversity, we need to keep finding ways to increase equity in decision-making in every level of every organization if that organization wants to succeed.

In the terms of creating equity by scaling conversations the focus is simply on the participants, not the questions. The questions are all of the things you need to make your organization successful. The equity portion is providing a platform for people's ideas to be shared and considered equitably regardless of who shared them.

Let's consider an area common to many organizations: The sales team.

Sales

If you want to increase the efficacy of all of your salespeople, ask them all for their thoughts on decisions that affect them. Simple. Rather than organize them in a hierarchy, here are questions that should be part of regular sales team cadence.

What is on your mind right now as a salesperson?
What do you want leadership to talk about at the monthly meeting?

What resources do you need to be successful in the next quarter?

What competitive intelligence do we most need to win right now?

What are some customer stories we all most need to hear right now?

What advice do you have for leadership as we plan for next year?

What are some of the biggest lessons from this quarter?

What are your thoughts and questions about the plan for this quarter?

Institutionalizing inclusion on revenue teams is a powerful way to showcase the power of equitable input. In one organization Thought-Exchange worked with, a leader wanted to understand why the lowest performing team was the lowest performing team. To do that, the leadership asked everyone on the team what skills and resources they felt they were lacking. They asked what information they needed to win. By ensuring all people's voices were heard in an equitable way, and appropriate actions were taken, that team transformed from the lowest to the highest over the course of one year.

Revenue teams are inspiring to work with because success can be easily measured in terms of increased effectiveness. Measuring people in sales is easier than measuring people in most other roles. Working to equitably remove barriers for your sales team to win showcases the power of scaling conversations to address equity. Rather than fixing problems for an elite few, the power is learning what matters most to the group as a whole and uncovering powerful common ground. When it is understood more broadly that an equitable approach to increasing revenue by decreasing bias equals more revenue, you have a situation similar to the electric car. Once it is the easy choice, not just the right choice, change will happen fast across all teams in all sectors.

Tackling equity on a grander societal and cultural scale poses additional challenges. Let's look at educational equity.

Equity in Education

The process of creating equity in education is a multi-generational journey that will likely not be completed inside the span of our lifetime. The systems that created the inequity were intentional and thorough. The dismantling of systems that don't provide equitable access to learning takes grit.

Earlier we addressed the survival brain reaction to new information and how that system fights to preserve our sense of self. That survival brain reaction is dominant in conversations about equity. When people make a claim that an educational system is not equitable, and is instead systemically racist, the reaction of the leaders, mostly white men, is often a survival brain-based response that systemic racism is simply not possible in such a caring and established community organization.

Only stark examples help illuminate the situation.

In one school system several members of the administration and board were adamant that systemic racism was not occurring. Yet a simple example existed that helped provide a pathway to discovering the many others.

Job placement programs were a tenet of the district as high school seniors were placed into internships at local organizations to help prepare them for college and career life. The only caveat? The student needed to own a car to be a part of the program. In that city, only one generation ago home ownership was next to impossible for a Black person as the banks had regulations prohibiting lending to Black clients, regardless of their income. This resulted in a wealth gap that meant in the next generation, very few Black families in the district had accumulated the wealth required for their kids to own cars. But a policy is a policy. And the result of that policy was that Black students couldn't participate in job placement. Until that policy is dismantled, progress won't happen.

Black students are also in most studies found to be more than twice as likely to be expelled from school after exhibiting similar bad behavior to their white peers. That coincides with the dramatically higher number of unarmed Black people shot by police officers compared to white citizens.

With all of these well-documented findings, I have still had several conversations with my white male peers. After I acknowledge my white privilege, the conversation sounds like this:

"You say I'm a privileged white man but you have no idea where I come from or what I have been through!"

Then I say some version of this:

"Ah! That's OK, you just don't understand. White privilege isn't about the hardship you didn't experience when you were a kid. You could have any background and you could have suffered any amount of trauma. Your white privilege is the color of your skin. You don't have people cross the street because the color of your skin threatens them. You don't have a harder time renting out an AirBnb because of your profile picture. You don't have a parent denied a loan because of the color of their skin. You aren't more likely to be shot by a police officer than your white neighbor. Your male white privilege is the fact that you are a white male."

Then they say: "Hmmm. Never thought of it that way."

The reason I point that out is that I believe systemic change will come out of a belief of optimizing a system based on understanding the raw power of equity in decision-making, not because white men the world over will suddenly agree this is a great idea. The experience of the results of equitable decision-making, like increased test scores, graduation rates and college graduations will then help create more equity champions. The unconscious bias and survival brain of many or most well-intentioned white leaders gets in the way of them learning about their own role in the problem.

The best questions about equity in education, again, are not questions about equity and are instead questions about the education system asked in an equitable way:

What are your thoughts about this change?

What is working well and what resources do you need?

What are your thoughts and questions about this funding scenario?

What are the most important skills and attributes of a graduate of our system?

What are some things we need to do to address teacher workload?

What is working well and what changes could be made to improve remote learning?

As a student, what are your thoughts on what teachers and administrators need to do more of to make more students successful?

These questions asked in an equitable manner have the power to change the world. A district ThoughtExchange worked with asked a student voice question similar to the last one and found the answers mapped extremely well to some of the most recent and sought-after research on learning put out by major universities. Teacher as facilitator, education on finding and discerning sources of truth, soft skill enhancement for STEM tracks. Simply by asking the students they uncovered actionable best practice learning methodologies in the language of their students.

In another more painful scenario, a New York State superintendent had reacted very quickly after the mass school shooting in Parkland, Florida. Parents and teachers were terrified the world over and to react to the moment the school board in this New York district hired armed foot patrols to provide protection on campus. After this was done, the superintendent scaled a conversation to ask everyone in the community for their thoughts and questions about the initiative. Many answers were what he expected. But some were not. Though only a small percentage of the school population identified as Black, a few parents shared powerful thoughts about their new fear of their students now potentially being shot in school for getting in a fistfight. History and stats proved their fears to be founded. These thoughts were not shared frequently but they resonated with the community and were elevated to the top of the conversation.

The superintendent took a humble approach to his response. He publicly apologized for this rash decision and admitted his own inherited biases kept him from considering how this decision would affect so many of his parents who are impacted by systemic racism. The conversation results were shared with many local officials and the decision to hire the armed officers was immediately reversed. Other safety precautions that didn't threaten young people of color were implemented.

In that same district, several months later a question was asked of parents to share what was on their mind for their school leadership to respond to. Right near the top was a thought about the frustrations of a Black mother who articulated that the burden of educating students about the historical and current impacts of racism should not fall on the shoulders of her children and should instead be the responsibility of the other parents and the system itself.

Notice in both of these cases, a normal operational question was asked in an equitable manner that protected and elevated the voice of people who needed to be heard. The conversation wasn't about equity. The conversation was about education and the platform was equitable.

****

The power of inclusive voice is already bearing fruit in balance sheets and measured outcomes of the organizations we lead. It is my belief we can apply these tools to include the voice of everyone: in politics, in business, in climate change, and in healing the divide between people caused by the short-term, individualist, survival-mode of our brains and our species.

From the earliest days of humanity we have experienced the value of leaning into our unique ability to collaborate and converse across kin groups to make the world more livable for all of us. And perhaps more importantly, we've learned as a species that conversation has the power to unlock the higher levels on the hierarchy of our needs. Rather than living in a continuous loop, stuck in safety and refinement of basic structures, our ability to converse with one another allows us to move up through our needs of alignment and shared culture toward our self-actualizing ideals of realizing vision and transformation. Ultimately, as the Blackfoot teach us, this leads, not to personal glory, but rather toward multi-generational continuity.

The skill of bringing people together, from anywhere on the globe, into scaled conversations in real time and in any language, is the new leadership competency. Whether you are a business executive or a public leader, building a better world for the people you are entrusted to serve will only be successful if you include them in the conversation.

Notes

1. https://www.nationalgeographic.com/science/phenomena/2013/01/31/the-real-wisdom-of-the-crowds/#close
2. https://www.npr.org/sections/money/2015/08/07/429720443/17-205-people-guessed-the-weight-of-a-cow-heres-how-they-did

ACKNOWLEDGMENTS

This book, and its author, are the product of a life of unearned advantages provided by being raised in a unique way by principled and deeply loving parents in traditional Secwepemc territory and encountering many people who imparted powerful ideas into my world-view. A common and noble declaration of those who seek to improve businesses and society is that their work is to plant trees whose shade they will never sit in. In considering the acknowledgments of this book I was happy to spend time reflecting on what made it possible while sitting in the shade of the trees planted by those who came before me.

The best way to understand how I grew up is to imagine you unexpectedly dropped by our small house in a small town in the middle of British Columbia, Canada, at dinner time. If the door wasn't already open, someone opens it when you ring the doorbell. Maybe it would be one of my two genetically related sisters, maybe any one of my several unrelated neurodiverse brothers and sisters my parents also cared for, maybe a friend or cousin living with us, or maybe an elderly neighbor.

Regardless of who opens the door, they lead you to the kitchen where ten to 20 people are eating together. As you approach, somehow the table magically extends and there's a chair for you, and enough food, as if my mom knew you were coming. You try to say you don't need to eat but it doesn't work. As you fill your plate with casserole and fresh salad from the garden, you look around the table and see a young First Nations girl clapping and hooting, a smiling young man with an autism tick, and a rancher with a hook replacing an arm he lost in the war. And this is just any old Tuesday. If it was Wednesday, it was pancake night.

My parents were both special education teachers and I grew up alongside all sorts of neurodiverse people. After visiting my home you might ask me, as hundreds of people have: "What's it like growing up in a home with so many brothers and sisters and different people around all the time?" My answer was some variation of this: "What's it like for you having hands? Well, that's what it's like for me. It's just a thing that's part of me and I love it."

That dinner table was for me the exact center point of the universe. As I got older, I was surprised to learn the whole world didn't grow up that way. I also came to recognize how privileged I was to be surrounded by so many amazing people in a house that always had enough food on the table.

My first steps out of that house were toward Educo Adventure School with charismatic and wise humans like Executive Director Ron Skene and his colorful cast of outdoor-adventuring characters, many of whom became mentors and then lifelong friends. Much of how I learned to see the world as a teenager was derived from a group of people who had a common belief in the power of drawing forth the best from young people through experiential education and group facilitation while visiting mountains and rivers throughout British Columbia.

During my time there, among the high ropes and climbing wall of the off-grid school site, a new and important structure was created annually by Caucasian allies Dylan Spencer, Kevin Skelcher, Erin Beagle, Jesse Sullivan, and many others under the careful guidance, love and support of David Balcaen, Anne Dunn, John and Eva McCarvill, Secwepemc Elder Johnny Johnson, Chief Mike Archie, and other local First Nation leaders who generously shared the gifts of their society and culture which has been successfully supporting the mental health and transformation of young people since time immemorial. The structure was the sweat lodge, and the lessons about voice and respect, and multi-generational continuity, were deeply impactful to me. When my father died suddenly and unexpectedly in his fifties, the sweat lodge was the first place I turned to grieve.

After leaving Educo, as a young entrepreneur I worked with and learned from incredible humans like Dino Vittorio and Rob Wishart as I carved out a living supporting neurodiverse young people while inventing a leadership business with Kevin Skelcher. Along the way I was fortunate to get advice and generous support from business leaders like Derek Welbourn, CEO of Inhaus Surfaces Limited and Antarctic, Everest and Pole to Pole expedition guide and meditation trainer Martyn Williams.

Delving into community development in my late twenties gave me the chance to learn from facilitators and community development leaders including Chris Corrigan, Kris Archie, Lea Smirfitt, Maria Mazzotta, and Rose Soneff, who each exposed me to new ways of understanding how to help people connect better with one another.

As you'll read in the body of this book, my work in analog community development facilitation had me connect with the catalyst Lee White, once Executive Director of Outward Bound Canada, who introduced me to someone who would become my mentor, boss, business partner, and close friend: Jim Firstbrook. He and his ex-CEO from CREO, Amos Michelson, exposed me to the thinking and experience of what was needed to build a technology company with a culture and product that could scale to include the passion and effort of thousands of people.

Condensing a decade of experience in the facilitation, outdoor, and community development space and blending it with distilled insight from a decade as a leader of a fast-growth conversation technology company has made me realize just how many incredible and sharp people I have been fortunate to learn from.

Rather than attempt to name everyone I have worked shoulder-to-shoulder with in recent years, I will restate what we have been pointing out together as an organization: All of us are better, smarter, and more articulate than any one of us. My honor is simply to curate. The many, many creative employees, investors, mentors, customers, and partners I have learned from in the last ten years have each uniquely helped me gather and shape these ideas about scaling conversations into a tight form that can now neatly fit into a book. For that, and for the shade of all of the efforts of all those who came before me, and for Shawna: Thanks.

About the Author

Dave MacLeod is an old-school facilitator, a proud father, an aspiring anti-racist co-conspirator, and the CEO and co-founder of the fast-growth conversation technology company ThoughtExchange .com. Dave and team work with leaders in large private and public organizations to help them access their unheard majority and bring unbiased voice to decision-making. Millions of people have been included in critical conversations on the ThoughtExchange platform. Prior to ThoughtExchange Dave was not in tech, and was instead a serial entrepreneur who designed businesses and events focused on analog group communication innovation.

LinkedIn: https://www.linkedin.com/in/dave-macleod-te

INDEX